FIRST SIGHT OF THE DESERT

FIRST SIGHT
OF THE DESERT

Discovering the Art of Ella Peacock

Kathryn J. Abajian

Kathryn J Abajian (signature)

THE UNIVERSITY
OF UTAH PRESS
Salt Lake City

For Gillmer

Printed on acid-free paper. Printed in China by C&C Offset Printing Company.

10 09 08 07 06 05   5 4 3 2 1

The Defiance House Man colophon is a registered trademark of
The University of Utah Press. It is based upon a four-foot-tall
Ancient Puebloan pictography (late PIII) near Glen Canyon, Utah.

Some parts of *First Sight of the Desert* were previously published as articles
in a different form in *Dialogue: A Journal of Mormon Thought* and in *Catalyst*.

Excerpt by Pat Mora from *Chants* is reprinted with permission of the publisher,
Arte Público Press—University of Houston.

Excerpts by Wendell Berry from "At a Country Funeral" in *The Selected Poems of
Wendell Berry*. Reprinted courtesy of Wendell Berry.

LIBRARY OF CONGRESS CATALOGING-IN-PUBLICATION DATA
Abajian, Kathryn J.
First sight of the desert : the life and art of Ella Peacock / Kathryn J. Abajian.
    p. cm.
Includes bibliographical references.
ISBN 0-87480-799-9 (pbk. : alk. paper)
1. Peacock, Ella Smyth, 1905-1999—Criticism and interpretation. 2. Utah—In art. I. Title.
ND237.P267A83 2005
759.13—dc22   2004012477

Frontispiece: *Ella Peacock* by Mark Andersen. Reprinted courtesy of Mark Andersen.

PUBLICATION OF *First Sight of the Desert* IS MADE POSSIBLE IN PART BY
A GENEROUS GRANT FROM THE CHARLES REDD CENTER FOR WESTERN STUDIES
AT BRIGHAM YOUNG UNIVERSITY.

CONTENTS

PROLOGUE

First Sight of the Desert evolved slowly into its final form. It began in my simple curiosity about an intriguing woman. Yet when I started to write Ella's life as a biography, I kept hearing the same questions from anyone who read or heard me read from early drafts: "Why are *you* so interested in her? What is it about Ella Peacock that *you* like so much?"

An attraction to Ella Peacock seemed obvious to me. Here was a woman completely unassuming yet so remarkable. It seemed logical that I should document her life in a traditional biography filled with her personal details and her art. In fact, to that point I'd consciously avoided including my reflections on Ella's experiences and purposely drew no conclusions.

Still, those recurring questions nagged me, telling me that others perceived something below the surface of my own project that I was completely oblivious to. Eventually, I heard the questions so many times that I began to pay attention.

Over the years of my visits to Sanpete County, I came to know Ella as a woman who had already realized her ambition, a woman with set habits of mind, a woman closing her life. As I looked back, I saw that during the years I researched her life, my entire world, in contrast, had been transforming—on multiple levels. I was leaving a marriage, living alone for the first time, going back to school for a graduate degree, changing from high school to community college teaching, and slowly withdrawing from a church I'd known for thirty years.

In the beginning I thought this personal revolution was independent from my new relationship with Ella; I had merely seen my research into her life as an academic pursuit, an exercise seated in my own intellect and in a need to document something important.

Now I understand that I was attracted to Ella Peacock and her life story *because* of her interior sovereignty, because of the very fact of her purposeful existence—solitary and seemingly content living in a desert valley. And I didn't know then, because I'd lived too long on the surface of my own emotions, that I was really seeking to know myself better through my understanding of her, hoping to awaken an identity I had once suppressed.

Like many others, I loved her paintings and enjoyed her eccentricity, but I realize now that in driving across the Nevada desert to Utah that first summer, I had really been driving toward myself, toward the person I was meant to become.

Writing about my quest, however, was not as easy as writing about Ella's, or what I perceived to be Ella's. Even so, the writing provided a way to ground my thoughts and to work out my own direction. The hard part was learning to be deliberate and contemplative, behavior that required huge expanses of solitude and caused me eventually to embrace the very loneliness I sensed in Ella.

Ultimately, I found the truest way to tell Ella's story was to speak about finding my own experiences illuminated through hers as I searched to discover why it is we lose our true selves so easily in the world, how it is that we so quickly forget who we once were.

> *Nothing you ever read about them can make you*
> *know them until you go there.... Never mind people*
> *who tell you there is nothing to see in the places where people*
> *lived who interest you! You always find something of what*
> *made them the souls they were and at any rate, you see*
> *their sky and their earth.*
>
> —Sarah Orne Jewett, correspondence with
> American artist Sara Whitman

Mt. Peacock. OIL, 20″ X 16″. COURTESY OF THE AUTHOR.

MT. PEACOCK

A person's life purpose is nothing more than to rediscover,
through detours of art, or love, or passionate work, those one or
two images in the presence of which his heart first opened.
—ALBERT CAMUS, *L'Envers et L'Endroit*

I NOTICED THE SMALL PAINTING as soon as I walked into her studio. I could actually feel desire stirring in my fingers as I picked it up.

"I painted that in Nevada in the 1930s," Ella told me, her voice sounding filled with some of the same wonder I was feeling. "I call it *First Sight of the Desert*. There were more, but that's the only one I have left from my trips west."

The painting was merely twelve by nine inches, yet the small canvas somehow contained the desert's stunning vastness, captured the delicacy of sagebrush and the sensuousness of sand. It was a hope-filled image of a land that had, until that moment, seemed desolate to me.

As Ella talked on, randomly gesturing toward the rest of her art haphazardly stacked everywhere in her studio, I traced the rough surface of the painting's frame with my fingertips, stroking the groove she had hand-carved into the wood. The frame was toned with a thin wash that somehow combined all the colors from the painting without replicating any one exactly. Soft light illuminated the foreground, pure and optimistic radiance. The dry, dusty landscape was filled with pastel colors beneath a clear, brilliant green-blue sky. I knew immediately I wanted to own it.

Oblivious to my longing, Ella led me about, showing me the many plein air paintings in her studio—propped on chairs and on her tattered beige sofa like guests waiting to be introduced, stacked against the walls two and three layers deep. She pointed to one with a sky that bothered her, another she called a "floperoo," one or two she wanted her son to have, others bare in stretched canvases waiting for her to carve their frames, some missing only her signature.

Holding *First Sight of the Desert,* the small treasure as I had already come to think of it, I realized its rarity among Ella's other paintings, its notable difference from the subdued palette of the rest of her work. The skies in the paintings crowding her studio were more complex, less calm, the sage a dusty blue-green, the mountains ocher. I was drawn into this quiet palette as well, to its simplicity and depth—qualities that seemed more fitting to the woman standing next to me.

Thin and angular, her long muscles well worn, Ella stood tall for an eighty year old. The practicality of her flannel shirt, khaki slacks, and no-nonsense manner seemed to leave space around her for the simple beauty she generated.

I looked around her studio and living room to see only grayed greens and creamy earth tones, colors infusing the walls of her home, her clothing, and, as was suddenly apparent to me when I left, the entire world outside her door and beyond the town in the desert of central Utah.

◈◈◈

Long before that summer afternoon when I fell so completely for Ella Peacock and that small painting, I'd been in the same part of Utah, in Sanpete County, enduring yet another one of many obligatory visits to my husband's family. That July, as always, the days were tolerably warm and dry, but the nights were suffocating.

Lying in one of the large lumpy beds that filled three small attic rooms crowded together at the top of a narrow staircase, I listened, wide-eyed, to the snuffling, sleep-talking, dream-whimpering of my children, all of it backgrounded by my husband's droning snore. The smells from the surrounding farms seeped up and into our slumber. Lying as close as I could to a tiny window that opened only a few inches, I longed for a cool breeze and waited for sleep.

My three children were small then, the oldest eight and the youngest two. We were visiting their grandparents in Fairview, an old farming town originally settled by Scandinavian converts to the Church of Jesus Christ of Latter-day Saints (LDS). Fairview seemed a highly optimistic, even fanciful, name for the place. A two-hour drive south of Salt Lake City, it was embedded in landscape that, to me at least, seemed godforsaken. In the mid-1800s, the Mormon prophet Brigham Young had sent groups of the faithful to such wild country throughout the state to claim and tame the land and establish communities.

My husband's family home was a tall brick building built in 1908. Formerly a bishop's storehouse, it once held the local Mormons' offerings, their tithes in the form of goods—mindfully donated wheat, alfalfa, and corn. In the late 1920s, the building had been converted to a residence. My husband was born there, on the same dark-green chenille sofa his parents continued to use in the living room, its walls still covered with 1940s-era wallpaper, dusty pink flowers splashed on a beige ground.

His elderly parents lived entirely in two large high-ceilinged rooms downstairs. They pulled out the sofa bed to sleep on each night and used the coal-fueled stove in the kitchen to cook their meals and heat the main floor throughout the bitter winters. They did their laundry in a 1930s Maytag wringer-washer next to the coal stove in the kitchen; the gray water was piped through the kitchen door directly onto the front lawn. Once in a while they drove their black 1946 Chrysler to the neighboring town to visit relatives or, more rarely, one hundred miles north to see a doctor in Salt Lake City.

The next morning we all ate breakfast around their oilcloth-clad round oak table in the center of the big kitchen. I was loathe to let my children drink the raw milk set on the table in an old-fashioned glass dairy bottle, so their father agreed to walk to the mercantile down the street for pasteurized low-fat milk safely sealed in a cardboard carton.

After breakfast, the high altitude and previous night's restlessness overwhelmed me. I dozed on the sofa while the children played outside, swinging on a rope hanging from the rafters of the old barn, chasing ducks in the neighbor's yard, and later shouting in the dusk gathering against the Wasatch Mountain range on the east side of Sanpete Valley.

My husband visited with relatives, telephoned some old friends, and late in the afternoon drove to Mt. Pleasant to visit his high school football coach. I waited out my dutiful time, comfortless in the disquieting emptiness of his family home and this small town.

Separated by thirty-five miles from Indianola, the closest town to the north, and six miles from Mt. Pleasant to the south, Fairview sits alone in the middle of the wide Sanpete Valley that stretches for desolate miles on the Wasatch Plateau of the Rocky Mountains. It is a barren, sage-filled space inhospitable to people and barely nourishing to cattle. I was unsettled by the intimidating summer storm clouds abruptly exploding in the distance and apprehensive about the proximity of the sunbaked desert just outside town. I could barely drink enough water to feel hydrated.

I had grown up in Southern California where the ocean's moist breezes were easily reached within an hour's drive south on Beach Boulevard; the big movie theaters and department stores of Los Angeles were but a few exits down the San Bernardino Freeway. We were raising our children in a tree-filled community in northern California, thirty miles from San Francisco and close enough to the ocean to enjoy its vigor frequently.

As a young mother, my purpose was singular, the measure of my industry confirmed in my children's physical and religious growth. I had ascribed to a particular way of life by choosing Mormonism when I was eighteen and by marrying in my early twenties. Even though I knew I was less devoted to the doctrine than to the easily measured lifestyle of the Mormon Church, I was committed to upholding its teachings.

But here in Sanpete County, feeling displaced in such a peculiar environment, I wondered at the ability of a geographic place—of natural landforms and atmospheric conditions—to arouse such qualms. After all, thousands of Mormon settlers had dedicated their lives to turning this seeming desolation into farmland and fulfilling Brigham Young's initial hope of making the "desert blossom as the rose," as the Book of Isaiah prophesies. But my familiar purpose as a woman seemed empty here, and I found myself questioning practices I'd long taken for granted. All I could see in Sanpete County, in the exact center of Utah, were miles of uncertainty and impossibility.

In fact, I'd learned all I wanted to know about Fairview during a visit the first year I married. My new husband and I had taken a walk one evening around the few buildings in town—the church, the "Merc," the post office, and the school. Completely at home there, he'd wanted me to appreciate his birthplace. He must have related many stories of his childhood, but all I remembered were startling anecdotes—a ten-year-old friend who lost his hand in a tractor accident, so many girls who left school pregnant, his non-Mormon neighbors who were considered odd, and poor families living in dugout basements because they had run out of money before they could build the ground floors of their homes.

He'd told me about the summer he worked in the turkey plant, standing in blood up to his shins, another summer that he threshed barley and broke out in hives, another when he walked five miles each way to the neighboring town to work on his aunt's farm for fifty cents a day. He remembered watching old westerns in the "picture-show house," a building converted from a former dance hall. And he talked of learning to swim late on hot summer nights at the local swimming hole.

All of it sounded irregular to me—interesting because of its novelty, but privately disturbing. I was sure I did not want to raise my children anywhere near that turkey plant and those dugouts. I didn't want them swimming without lifeguards or drinking milk that arrived on the doorstep still warm. And I had, I realized, a palpable fear of becoming the sort of wife who would fit easily in such a place.

The town was so quiet. It came alive only on Sunday mornings or during the Friday-night "Dime-a-Dip" dinners held in the church basement, meals that regularly featured casseroles garnished with potato chips, sugary Jell-O salads, and desserts smothered in Cool Whip. During Sunday services, clerical announcements were routinely corrected or amended aloud, usually by an older man in the congregation. Hymns celebrating the early Mormons' steadfast and perilous treks across the plains droned on haltingly. The families sitting in the wooden pews, so used to one another and their ways, seemed indifferent to an energy I trusted and to a certain upbeat enthusiasm for the faith found readily in my California congregation. I didn't know who I was in this Mormon community. I began to doubt my own identity, a construct that suddenly seemed of my own making, cloistered and increasingly fragile.

Sitting in those pews, a lone brunette in what seemed an entire congregation of blondes, I felt conspicuous. I completely believed the local joke about Sanpete County's Scandinavian heritage: When the bishop asked, "Will Brother Larsen offer the benediction?" five men stood ready to pray. After he clarified, "Brother Lars

Larsen, please," two sat down. Residents who had lived in the town for twenty years were still called "newcomers." The local newspaper, the *Pyramid,* announced our arrival that week in its society section, calling us "visitors from California," as though we came from a faraway land.

A small town's celebrated sense of community seemed elusive to me there, the town's silence somehow secretive—as though the sky and the steep mountain ranges sealed this place off from the rest of the world. Yet the animal life—the horses, cows, and swooping hawks, with their snorts and lows and sharp cries—was immediate and inescapable. Tractors working the sandy soil seemed to me to be engaged more usefully and intimately than anything that could happen between any two people there.

It was on such an afternoon of boredom and disorientation in 1985 that I had met Ella Peacock and her art for the first time. The parched air again made everything still and eerily calm. For some diversion from perfunctory conversation on yet another visit to my husband's home in Fairview, I took a short drive south on Highway 89. After I passed through Mt. Pleasant, I spotted a faded sign advertising Horseshoe Mountain Pottery and veered left onto a small road that wound southeastward. A cluster of buildings appeared, and an old wooden marker announced, "Welcome to Spring City, a National Historic District Founded in 1852."

I slowed down on Main Street, apparently the town's only paved road, and, passing a small gas station and Strate's dry goods store, came upon Horseshoe Mountain Pottery. Its storefront was vintage pioneer construction, weathered wood with a coat of peeling deep-red and dark-yellow paint.

Inside the small store, narrow wooden shelves held large and small bowls, platters, and cups. The potter's wheel filled the second half of the interior, along with pots in various stages of completion, stacks of newspapers for packaging purchases, children's art, and tools—all covered in fine clay dust. I admired a painting of a woman, her stylized figure portrayed in intense colors, hanging above the counter.

The messiness of the shop, its undercurrent of disorder and absentmindedness, made me immediately comfortable. It recalled my undergraduate days tramping around the aged brick buildings of Brigham Young University's Lower Campus as an art student, washing brushes in big old porcelain sinks, dragging stools across worn wooden floors, splattering clay on my clothes.

I told the owner how remarkable it was to find such lovely art and pottery in this small town. The potter, Joe Bennion, a man with an intense gaze and full beard, smiled and told me Spring City was a sort of artists' colony and began naming painters living within pointing distance of his shop, including Ella Peacock, whose house was just diagonal from his pottery.

A few minutes later, I walked across the street and was standing on the driveway under the large fir trees that shaded the whole of that house just as Ella opened her front door. Her Chesapeake retriever darted past her and ran toward Main Street.

"Jeffery, Jeffery, come right back here!" she admonished him sharply.

Standing tall in men's work clothes, her long white hair knotted in back and secured with a headband, Ella seemed formidable, with an air of craggy authority. Yet she invited me into her 125-year-old adobe house that summer afternoon—into her paintings and her life.

As I walked through her doorway, an arresting pungency of oil paint and turpentine vied for my attention with a remarkable hand-painted border encircling the walls of two rooms. Rendered in fading earth colors on the dove-gray walls, the waist-high border frieze depicting Native American icons provided a subtle depth of character to her home. It was as though a designer had carefully readied it for a museum exhibit of western art.

Large-scale portraits—bold narratives of self-assured women—filled her living room walls. In her adjacent studio, smaller paintings surrounded her easel and stool, filling the room with quiet imagery of the desert landscape; paint splatters punctuating the worn wooden floor and shop lights hanging from the ceiling sang out her devotion to her work. Near an antique desk, a set of parched deer antlers was framed in a foot-deep window alcove. I was captivated by the understated artfulness and felt unexpectedly at home.

When she showed me her current work, her many paintings of the desert, I completely connected. I was drawn to their simplicity, to images of a land I'd never valued, a landscape I had actually scorned during the previous fifteen years of my summer visits to Utah with my family.

Ella painted a land I eventually came to love—the high desert of the Great Basin, a land often referred to as a vast, salty nothingness, the least appreciated of North America's deserts. In this forbidding basin between high mountain barriers, plants work hard to adapt and continually struggle to conserve water, as is usual in arid places.

But the Great Basin is entirely unlike Arizona's Sonora Desert with its impressively large saguaro cacti; dissimilar, too, are southern Utah's dramatic red-rock canyon lands, known for their colorful, showy sandstone, dramatic buttes, and labyrinthine canyons.

Sanpete County's western desert is seldom a destination for travelers. Here the vista is utterly sun-faded and horizontal, its appeal not immediately certain. Overgrazing has destroyed all but the most persevering vegetation, such as the omnipresent Great Basin sagebrush.

Yet Ella had found the singular beauty in this land. Her work gave weight to the faded, sun-parched colors and value to the ordinary sage. These paintings, tucked and stacked everywhere, attested to a certain and patient watchfulness, documents of her encounters with an unassuming and overlooked power in the land.

Distinguished by a gentle, reserved palette and loose brush strokes, her 1920s style both dated her work and attracted me to it. I had always been intrigued by the social history of the twenties and thirties, a time when the art sensibility seemed to be more purposeful and practical than that informing most contemporary art. Ella's work reflected that deliberate consciousness.

The small painting *First Sight of the Desert* stood out from the others, its colors more vibrant and somehow younger. Still holding it, I told her how much I'd like to own one of her paintings. "I don't want to sell that one," she warned quickly. "I want to keep it here."

"Do you have any for sale?" I asked.

"Oh, there might be one or two," she hedged.

I asked about a larger one leaning against the wall, a landscape in her signature subdued colors, showing a gently sloping mountain with a thick stand of sagebrush in the foreground. I was attracted to the mellow blue-green of the sage and the soft curves of the tawny mountain that dominated the work's temperamental sky. The paint, applied sparingly in broad brush strokes, revealed the texture of the canvas in places.

"That's *Mt. Peacock*. That's what I named the mountain when I painted it. Nobody knows that, of course. That spot is just below Manti, near Nine Mile Pond. I can do that, you know. Change things. But I can't sell that to you. It's not finished. I need to work on that corner of the sky, and I'm not sure the frame is right."

We talked for a few more minutes about the desert and her love of it. At last she acquiesced—agreed to finish the painting of Mt. Peacock, sign it, and have it ready for me the next day.

That summer afternoon in Ella Peacock's home, as I watched her sun-spotted, gnarled hands hold her paintings with such a light touch, I had that feeling of falling instantly in love. It seemed as though everything around me suddenly made sense— this woman, her house and her art, the stunning landscape, all easing into one harmonious chord.

Leaving her that afternoon to contemplate "that corner of the sky" in *Mt. Peacock,* I walked out into a day that seemed somehow less unsettled, into a town less strange. I didn't know it then, but I was ready for someone like Ella. I drove away from Spring City that day newly attentive, believing I had just met a woman who realized her purpose and who seemed to possess and inhabit her life fully—a woman doing what she wanted.

Grandfather's Portrait. OIL, 25″ X 30″. COURTESY OF JIM AND BETTY KLEZER.

GRANDFATHER'S PORTRAIT

*If there was a road, I could not make it out in the
faint starlight. There was nothing but land: not a country
at all, but the material out of which countries are made.*
—WILLA CATHER, *My Antonia*

I T WAS IN LATE JUNE 1991, six years after meeting Ella, that I dedicated my first
summer to researching her life. This time I came to Utah alone, spurred by the
draw of *Mt. Peacock* hanging above my living room sofa, art that brought the desert's
calm into my increasingly strained California home. The painting had silently enticed
me for years, drawing me toward a clear promise in its sloping desert mountains.

This was also the summer I decided to end my marriage. I'd waited too many
long, lonely years in a lifeless union, feeling as though I was finally leaving, as Eugene
O'Neill described, "something that died without ever having lived."[1] The final decision came full of dread, the final act a mix of deflation and energy.

Mine was a marriage without connection, a union that functioned on a practical
level only—merely accomplishing the perfunctory requirements of parenting, budg-
eting, shopping, attending church, catching movies, and watching ball games. There
hadn't been any shared partnership or common goals for decades.

I'd been leaving for years, I realized. At first it was only for an extra hour here and
there, then weekends, then weeks away when possible. I didn't leave en route to anything, had no destination, no goal or person I was replacing for my family home. I
just knew I regularly felt more at home away from home. If not for my strong bond
with my children, I would have left physically much sooner, taking the exit my heart
and mind had already chosen.

◆◆◆

That summer I drove to Utah full of guilt and fear and hope all at once. I had written Ella the previous winter, asking permission to investigate her life, thinking merely that there was something important there to note. At the time, I hadn't any idea that simple request would become a critical part of a large step away from my former life. And though I'd been unsure she would remember me since I'd visited her only a few times in the previous years, she responded quickly.

She closed her letter to me saying, "By the way, the reason I am here is that the first time I saw this area I knew I could paint the rest of my days here." The sense of contentment in that comment also pulled me toward her and toward a landscape that, I recognized only later, was layered with possibility.

My drive across Nevada was enlivening. The valleys lay meadowlike, graced with thickets of wildflowers after heavy winter rains, and I carried an optimism that grew with each mile I left behind me, surprised at a welcome sense of anticipation that helped diminish the anguish of my marital estrangement.

It was my first fully deliberate, self-directed trip to Utah in nearly twenty-five years, and I drove straight through from California to Salt Lake City in twelve hours, suffused with a certain readiness, a nearly adolescent excitement of leaving home for the first time.

It's about a one-hundred-mile drive from the ever-increasing congestion of Salt Lake to the pastoral openness of Sanpete County. Southbound on I-15, the main freeway that stretches the length of the state, passing the sprawl of homes and businesses along the Wasatch Front, I took the ramp for Highway 6 heading due east and then turned south through Spanish Fork Canyon.

Utah's wilderness nearly takes over at that point in the route, the land asserting itself in the undiminished vigor of sagebrush and dry, rocky terrain foregrounding spectacular Mt. Nebo, nearly twelve thousand feet tall. I drove alongside railroad tracks snaking below high rust-red canyon walls, then on the new road up Billy's Mountain that overlooks the jarring evidence of a natural disaster that devastated the tiny town of Thistle in 1983.

What remained of the town were lifeless artifacts—a hollowed-out red-rock schoolhouse, uprooted tree skeletons seemingly fossilized, roofs tossed onto hillsides. Here the land—heavy with spring moisture—had slid into the canyon, creating a temporary lake that inundated the town with fifty feet of mud and water.

After Thistle, the road descends into countryside that suddenly opens up into Sanpete Valley, a wide expanse of solitude. Alone in my car, I was where I wanted to be that morning, ironically stimulated by the vastness and motivated by the tranquillity.

I know now that I entered Ella Peacock's canvases as I drove into Sanpete Valley that day. But at the time, I felt only a warm sense of familiarity, some kind of knowledge of an important reality below the surface of the plain, sandy soil and scrubby plants. As I look back, I realize that I had been engaged in the same line of perspective Ella saw on the frequent jaunts she offhandedly referred to as "just looking" at the land. I passed places she had painted from inside her car summer and winter, usually parked in a ditch away from curious motorists.

Without seeing another car for miles in either direction, I watched as magpies pounced on roadkill and herds of horses grazed lazily. I felt vicarious pride in the scattered working farms and weather-beaten outsized barns leaning impossibly.

With my car windows wide open, I inhaled clean air, dry and redolent of the alfalfa, wheat, and corn growing in fields stretching to the foothills. I drove past sturdy old flour mills and granaries still in use, buildings whose great practicality Ella so admired.

In the distance, the snow-rimmed crater, called "the Horseshoe" by locals, marked the outlying skyline above the town of Spring City. Everywhere, after years of looking past it, I noted the ever-present, persistent sagebrush, *Artemisia tridentata,* growing along fence lines and surrounding the irrigated fields, existing frugally on hard ground.

All at once I grasped that this valley, whose worth I had overlooked for decades, had been feeding Ella Peacock's imagination for those same years—certainly long enough for her to compose her nearly complete paean to the desert's fortitude.

Just past Indianola I had to stop in the middle of the highway, amazed as at least a hundred sheep surrounded my car—bleating and confused as they crossed the road on their way to the mountains for the summer. After crossing the San Pitch River, I drove up Fairview Canyon Road, turned left as directed at a chain-link fence stuffed with old blue bottles, and headed up the dirt road that led to my friend Dan's sprawling ranch house where I was to stay for the next two weeks.

I was finally there, halfway between leaving and coming, on the border between the scatterings of my past and a future as yet formless, leaving the woman I'd been for so long and walking into the life of a woman I barely knew.

Each day during those two weeks, I made the relaxing fifteen-mile drive south from the Fairview ranch house to visit Ella in Spring City. One day about noon, after passing the large stone church in the middle of town, I saw Joe Bennion working in front of his pottery shop. He was adjusting a load of hay packed in the bed of his old pickup. "This is only part of what we'll need," he said. "It takes three hundred bales to feed our three horses every winter."

Even though I hadn't seen him in a year, Joe greeted me as though it had just been a few weeks since we'd last met. We talked about his work—both around his home and in the pottery. And we talked about the latest town controversy.

"The mayor wants to pave the dirt roads here, but a lot of people in Spring City don't want to spend the money," he explained with some irony. "There'll have to be a bond election, I'm sure."

Standing beside his truck in his farmer's overalls, his long ponytail and full beard the antithesis of the typical modern Mormon's clean-cut image, Joe's unconventionality was refreshing.

I left Joe to his work and walked over to Ella's house to find her in her side yard enjoying the early June sun. She sat on a tree stump, her aged and weathered skin blending chameleon-like with a four-foot-high woodpile scattered with deer antlers, twisted gray branches, and the bleached skeletons of sagebrush she had gathered from the desert. Dressed in her usual paint-splattered jeans, tennis shoes, and two men's shirts—one as a jacket over the other—Ella rested precisely where the sun hit, her long hair hanging damp and loose to catch its rays.

"Oh, you're here," she said as I startled her out of her daydream. "I'm just drying my hair. I washed it because the sun's out today." It was the first time I'd seen her with her silver-gray hair down instead of knotted behind her neck, the stray wisps held away from her face with her trademark headband made from scrap fabric.

She brought to mind the image of an old Ute Indian woman, something truly native to this place. In contrast to the desiccated heap of the woodpile, a hedge of lilacs bloomed lushly all along her property line in opulent bouquets of purple, white, and lavender. I chose another stump, joining Ella and her white cat named, as was her black one, Pussy Cat. From our vantage point in her side yard, we considered Ella's old adobe house.

"I liked this house as soon as I saw it, and so did Bill," Ella said. "We liked old places." Something about the unassuming structure must have spoken to her when she and her husband, Bill, bought it in 1968. They'd worked on it for two years before they moved in, and lived together in Spring City for ten years before Bill died.

Set at the corner of 300 South and Main Streets, Ella's Spring City house was constructed in the 1860s by a Danish immigrant, Lauritz Larsen, who built it with locally made adobe bricks in traditional pioneer "vernacular"-style architecture. The adobe walls were later plastered, then painted taupe and accented with brown trim around the windows and doors. Originally built over a spring with only two rooms— an attic and a stone cellar. The kitchen, dining room, and bath were added later in the 1930s.

Small and subdued, the house is sheltered beneath the deep green of fir and maple trees, their branches spread wide over the gray composition roof. "Golly, I repaired that roof myself after Bill died, got up there and hammered it," Ella said. I would learn, in fact, she could wield practically any tool. She took pride in her carpentry skills and made sure I knew she had the ability to live alone despite her obviously weakening strength and dexterity.

We walked around to the front of the house while Ella explained the practicality of her front porch, its floorboards supported by large blocks of limestone and protected by a deep overhang. She couldn't remember where she'd picked up the row of four antique theater chairs—the usual daybed for her two cats—that awaited visitors. But she warmed up to the topic of an old empty oil tank set horizontally on the porch and painted to resemble a covered wagon. It too had a story.

A man had one day stopped to ask Ella if she would sell the tank to him. He said he wanted to keep his wood in it. "I don't know whether he was pulling my leg or not. He seemed perfectly serious, but I couldn't imagine why he thought he could keep his wood in an oil tank!"

Ella had painted the oil tank soon after she and Bill moved to Spring City. The effort seemed to me to reflect a popular and frivolous craft—the embellishment of something utilitarian—that women's groups were fond of pursuing. It was a socially sanctioned use of a woman's time to decorate something useful, and I had trouble reconciling the Ella who might have once cared to do so with the Ella who had since filled hundreds of canvases.

Rounding the west side of her house, we encountered a wild patch of bright-red opium poppies with deep-black centers blooming between the house and her barn-like garage, its weather-beaten boards shimmering with slivers of captured sunlight. The shed built against the garage wall about fifteen feet from her back door held the coal Ella chopped to warm her winter-cold rooms.

I commented on some large, scraggly sagebrush, the only plants growing close to the house. "Bill and I brought those sagebrush plants here. We dug them up in the desert out by Pigeon Hollow Road and replanted them around the house." The soft tone of the wild, sprawling gray-green sage harmonized with the taupe plaster of her house. The plants clearly expressed her retort to conventional landscaping.

Everything about her property, a modest half-acre containing the old adobe house, the cavernous garage, and the woodpile, spoke to me of what I thought of as Ella's industry and contentment. I would soon learn how much the humble Spring City house in this remote valley of a western state contrasted with the grand house in Germantown, Pennsylvania, where on September 30, 1905, Ella Gillmer Smyth had been born.

◈◈◈

Later that week I rapped the tarnished brass knocker on Ella's old pioneer front door. I'd heard music as I walked up her driveway, and now the strains of *St. Cecelia's Mass,* played loudly enough to permeate the foot-thick adobe walls, muffled my knock. After a minute or two, I opened the door myself, trying not to startle Ella, who sat on her sofa clearly absorbed in the recording.

She stood abruptly when she noticed me, her eyes brightening, and announced, "I remembered you were coming, so I haven't lost all my marbles." She indicated her black photo album waiting on the Sheraton gate-legged table beside the TV. I nudged Pussy from her place on the tattered green sofa and turned on my tape recorder as Ella opened the book of her childhood. "I want to show you my people," she said.

The George and Adelaide Smyth family, fortified with their heritage of hard work and good fortune, was firmly established in Germantown and Philadelphia society when Ella Gillmer was born, the third child—after George Albert Jr. and Mary Adelaide. The blue-eyed, raven-haired Ella, called their "black Irish," enjoyed the indulgence afforded the "baby" before two more sisters were born when she was five, effectively making her a middle child. Caught then in a nearly impossible place between the competence of her older siblings and the charm of her baby sisters, Ella's long search for her own identity began.

Germantown was at the time an affluent urban village filled with brick houses and tree-shaded cobblestone streets lying six miles northwest of Philadelphia along Wissahickon Creek. Although it's not now the wealthy enclave it was when the Smyths lived there, Germantown today is still known for the carefully maintained abundance of eighteenth- and nineteenth-century architecture that typified the Smyths' neighborhood while Ella was growing up.

Ella's album contained a photo of the Smyth family home at 242 Harvey Street, a large three-story brick colonial with a Victorian-style steep-pitched roof and white gingerbread porch railing. It looked like the house I'd imagined for the characters in the books I'd read as a child, the sort required for an idyllic childhood.

Indeed, it seemed the Harvey Street house provided the ingredients for that model childhood. Ella remembered its screened porch where she slept with her siblings in the summer and sometimes even in the winter when they lowered the canvas awnings against the frigid air and donned wool caps. She told me about the four bedrooms for the children on the second floor, just below the maids' third-floor bedrooms and bath. The family's parlor held a piano and the latest in Victorian furniture.

A seamstress came to the house weekly to make and mend the gingham dresses and matching bloomers the Smyth girls wore to Quaker school. Ella talked fondly of a family relation, Wong Ho, who catered the Smyths' frequent dinner parties. But the children weren't permitted to eat with the adults. They ate separately and played in the cellar—the adults' music and laughter seeping down through the floorboards.

It appears that Ella's parents conscientiously provided their growing family with the security and comfort they could well afford. But their third child was not so easily accommodated and pacified; Ella's sense of displacement, which began early in her childhood, seemed to have lasted her lifetime. Often when we talked, Ella passionately recounted her childhood frustrations and fears as though with fresh offense.

In Ella's voice I heard the pain of the prevailing sense of helplessness she experienced as a child: "When I was a little girl, not even five years old, I'd sit under the drop-leaf table and wiggle the leg. One time I pulled one leg all the way in and the kerosene lamp on top fell over and spilled on the floor and rug. Boy, did I get bawled out." I pictured young Ella hidden away from the family bustle, pushing the limits of propriety, her dark head bowed, her large blue eyes wide with apprehension.

When Ella was five and her new sister replaced her as the baby, her mother wrote in Ella's baby book: "Ella stomped next door to her grandparents and demanded, 'Is *that* going to stay at my house?'" Her mother noted, "It was several months before Ella was reconciled to *that*."

Ella explained the complete lack of selfhood she felt growing up with her siblings, typical for a middle child. "My older sister, Mary, had full authority over me. I would have temper tantrums, and, she told me years later, she would purposely make me cry, then hold me by the shoulders until I shut up."

Ella's fragile stability collapsed dramatically when she was nearly six years old. She condensed the moment into a few sentences, recounted with a touch of pride: "Mother had just had another baby, Father his second nervous breakdown, my sister pneumonia, and I had just poured water on the piano keys. Aunt Dibbie asked what she could do to help, and Mother said, 'Take Ella!'" So Ella's maiden aunt Dibbie, who lived next door, cared for young Ella for six months.

Aunt Dibbie taught Ella to sew, and for the first time, Ella learned to calm her anxiety by using her hands purposefully and creatively. She remembered reclining contentedly on a window seat, her feet propped up, making pincushions out of felt scraps and cardboard for her father, who later assured her they were just what he needed. The object lesson probably ensured Ella's lifelong inventiveness, providing a direction to a serene place she would rediscover years later as a lonely widow in the West.

With the black album open on her bony knees that afternoon in Spring City, she turned the brittle pages carefully with her long fingers, the joints swollen in the early stages of arthritis. A photo fell to the floor, a snapshot of a painting. "That's Grandfather," she announced as I retrieved it. "I painted that when I was in art school and made the frame as well. But it was stolen from me."

The large twenty-five-by-thirty-inch portrait in a simple hand-carved gold-leafed frame depicted Ella's maternal grandfather, Leander Munhall, his authority and barely perceptible impatience rendered in deep neutral colors. His pose, half-turned away from a desk stacked with papers and books, suggested a man with a great deal on his mind and much more to accomplish.

"He was a lively man and my favorite grandparent," Ella explained. "I left the painting with my brother when I moved to Wayne County. When I asked for it back, my brother's daughter, Betsey, had it and refused to return it." Later I would learn that Ella's niece, who lives in New Jersey and calls herself Betty, treasures the painting of her great-grandfather that she believes she rightfully inherited from her father.

However, the "stolen painting" annoyed Ella her entire adult life. Her grandfather Munhall had openly favored Ella as a child, and she admired his exploits and adventures and thought of him with both affection and esteem. This lost painting represented her only remembrance of his approval and encouragement of her. In 1987 Ella had begun a fruitless ten-year letter-writing campaign to get the painting back. Her niece showed me the correspondence: the first letter demanded her niece return it; a year later Ella "understood" her niece's reluctance; the following year Ella hired a Provo lawyer to write, claiming her rightful ownership. She paid the lawyer with four paintings. The next year Betty's brother Bert wrote, pleading for family peace. At last, when Ella was ninety, her sympathetic friend Helen Madsen typed a one-page letter, a final entreaty. It was filled with corrections and inserted comments in Ella's handwriting.

The contested painting's subject, the Reverend Leander Whitcomb Munhall, was a complex man whose high moral expectations intermingled with a playful nature. But he was best known as a stern cleric who preached fundamentalist Methodism throughout the country and Europe. Other members of the Methodist clergy objected to his conservative theology, which they saw as obstinate in the face of a modernist movement in the Methodist Church.

Still, he dedicated his life to church service, continuing his appeal to church members for the renunciation of dancing, card playing, and theater attendance. A letter in the *Los Angeles Times* in 1886 criticized Dr. Munhall for his sermon that had reviled American women who "carry dogs and ignore their babies" and who had "stopped teaching their daughters to cook."[2] He was determinedly active and preached into his nineties.

As the family patriarch, living with his wife and daughter next door to the Smyths, Munhall absolutely disallowed smoking or drinking in his home, required nightly family prayer with the Smyth family, and prohibited knitting or cooking on Sundays. Yet he was also known for his humanity. Whenever he told the maids he was going out for a walk, they started cooking frantically. They knew that he would inevitably seek out homeless men who would return with him for a meal.

He enjoyed telling his grandchildren stories about himself that promoted a larger-than-life image. One concerned a Bible in his rucksack that stopped a Civil War bullet from killing him, but according to his great-grandson, the family historian Bert Smyth, it was really a wad of tobacco that had spared him. He entertained his grandchildren with tales of his rebellious nature as a child: the time he proudly walked home from a swimming hole stark naked because his mother had confiscated his clothes for swimming without permission, and the time, Ella remembered, he "hammered a nail through my sister's dress to keep her in place" when he was baby-sitting.

Grandfather Munhall sounded unyielding to me, a man used to having his way in his family and his congregation, not an uncommon privilege for men in the early

1900s during the years Ella came of age. Ella was clearly impressed with his power and, most likely, envious of his autonomy.

"Let me show you my mother," Ella said, getting up from the sofa. "I'll get her picture." She returned from her bedroom with a black-and-white photo of Adelaide Munhall Smyth framed in engraved silver. Her mother sat formally, a regal countenance with upswept hair, dressed in black taffeta with a starched white collar.

"I thought a lot of my mother, but she was often out of patience with me," Ella explained. "I'm sure she wished I were more like my older sister because Mary was a better person, more steady. Father brought us up to tell the truth. And I always spoke my mind, but Mother said she sometimes wished I hadn't been telling the truth. Listen, I know my mother thought I should be more like Mary. Mary did what she was supposed to. I guess I didn't."

The living room was cool inside the thick adobe walls—the early summer's heat held outside, the sun's slant barely revealed on the broad sills. Ella, I realized, had begun revealing her fears to me, pointedly exposing the source of her still-present self-doubt established when she was a child. It was an aspect of her character that clashed noticeably with the driven artist I was coming to know.

❖❖❖

"Tell me about school," I asked later that week.

"Oh, I couldn't stand school until the second grade. I was a nervous child," Ella explained. "I had double curvature of the spine and had to do exercises in a special gym."

Ella's aunts Hannah and Dibbie, her mother's sisters, homeschooled Ella through first grade. She was then enrolled in Germantown Friends School, a demanding and rigorous Quaker institution her sister attended in the heart of Germantown. In existence since colonial days, the school still claims its long-held mission "to develop students with the intellectual and spiritual power to make a difference in the world."[3] Ella's older brother, Albert, attended the Germantown Academy, a private boys' school founded in 1759. Both of these exclusive schools offered rigorous academics and had long waiting lists because of the poor quality of the Philadelphia public schools.

Ella admired the spartan environment of the Friends School, where students sat on old wooden benches "without heat or any other monkey business." This was an education students had to "earn or they didn't get a diploma," and those who graduated didn't need to apply to colleges and universities; they were accepted without entrance exams. It was a school that "didn't waste time on cooking and sewing," but required the study of Latin in addition to another foreign language. Ella spoke of her Quaker education with deep-seated approval, tacitly censuring most other educational systems.

But Ella's artistic nature resisted some of the discipline expected at the Germantown school. She often daydreamed during her classes and, as an elementary school child, began what would later become her full-time occupation: looking at the landscape. She remembered, "I wasn't a very good student. I remember one time particularly. They asked me a question, and I hadn't been paying attention. I hadn't heard the questions because I wasn't listening; I was often looking out the window. I thought I could imagine what the question was, so I answered it and they thought I was impudent, so I was sent to Master Stanley, the principal. He reprimanded me."

I laughed with Ella. Then we just sat quietly for a while watching Pussy Cat stretch and roll awake. The voice of the child Ella once was—spunky yet easily humbled—lingered, reminding both of us how little we change, how firmly we are established as children.

I think we both felt satisfied with our visit that afternoon; I'd learned so much, willingly transported back to the turn of the century, to times reduced to black-and-white simplicity, but to a place so much more complex, really, than I could discern from Ella's recollections. Although she was sometimes frustrated trying to summon the details of her past in order to answer my direct questions—she'd say, "My 'forget-tery' gets better every day!"—Ella often seemed relaxed, even secure, as she indulged in the stories implicit in the old photographs.

As I left late that afternoon, we agreed that I would come over the next day after she returned from painting and had watched *Days of Our Lives,* her favorite soap opera. "That's the loneliest time for me, the afternoons," she offered, as I opened the door to leave. I heard her at the time, but it would be years before I would fully understand that loneliness. In my state of blind admiration I saw only an independent and productive woman, a woman supporting herself with her art, a woman doing, I now realize, what I wanted to do.

Ella was putting an album on her record player as I closed the door. As I walked down her driveway, I could clearly hear her favorite pianist, Vladimir Horowitz, playing Chopin's Mazurka in A Minor, its liveliness working to lift her mood.

Driving back to Fairview Canyon that afternoon, I thought about Ella's childhood discomfort and restlessness. She felt she had never fitted in, felt misplaced in her hometown, her home state, everywhere in the high culture of the East. She had told me, "The people in Germantown gave afternoon teas and so on, and I didn't like living that way. Everyone in Germantown was self-centered, self-important. They say in New York, to be someone you had to have lots of money; in Philadelphia you had to have a very important background and family. I'll tell you, one's as bad as the other."

Years later when I traveled in Pennsylvania and upstate New York, I recognized the land she grew up in as claustrophobic as well, lush countryside but without sight lines, the dark green of the forest encroaching on the roadways. I understood how Ella would have connected the East Coast culture of correctness with its "too green" land, and I would come to understand how it motivated her desire to move west.

As I thought about her art and her preference for painting landscapes, I began to understand her struggles with portraiture. It wasn't hard to see that she preferred to explore open land rather than close relationships with people. Her comfort in solitude even as a young woman bespoke her aversion to society's drive for conformity and propriety.

Interestingly, many of the portraits Ella painted during the 1920s and 1930s, including *Grandfather's Portrait* and many in Spring City, often contained in one way or another a pointed discord, a quality absent in her landscapes. She talked to me with ease about these outdoor scenes, mostly chattering about her experiences on the location, such as the time she once painted for hours unaware in rattlesnake territory in Texas. She would readily point out the parts of a composition that she had invented (mountains usually) or removed (mostly unnatural "landscaping").

Yet she continually questioned her ability to make portraits and always commented on her feelings for the subject she painted, mixing these up with her view of the success or failure of the likeness.

Ella's tolerance of the company of people was limited, a fact that, it seemed, revealed itself in her problems painting them. Ella's difficulty capturing personality, something she and others occasionally attributed to her failing eyesight, was, I believe, partially attributed to her disinclination to get close to her sitter and by her failure to feel at home in the social world.

The art critic John Berger, discussing the encounter required between an artist and subject, points out that the portrait painter needs to collaborate with the model, to get close enough to forget "convention, reputation, reasoning, hierarchies, and self."[4] Ella, it seemed, could not work around those impediments. And she seemed unable to create the artifice and idealization that portraiture often calls for.

Her dilemma in capturing her mother on canvas is a case in point. "Mother was very difficult to paint because, when she posed, it was definitely a pose. I tried and struggled with it, but I never got a successful painting." Ella's relationship with her mother was likewise difficult: whereas her mother valued a degree of social posing, Ella resisted it completely.

During the 1930s she tried painting her younger sister Jane, one of two sisters for whom Ella had conflicted feelings. Ella told me that she grew disappointed with the dark tone of the painting, acknowledging, "I kept pushing Jane into the shadows."

When I admired the large, almost regal depiction of a young Philadelphia horsewoman, Honey Ross, hanging in her living room, Ella disregarded my praise. Instead, she confessed—still guilty nearly seventy years later—that she had sold the painting to Honey Ross for fifty dollars, but after subsequently borrowing the work for a Philadelphia exhibit, she never contacted Ms. Ross to return the painting. "Now I don't know what to do," she worried, sounding as though a solution could still be found.

Ella often mentioned a portrait she painted in art school of John Laurence Wetherill, "a lawyer from a top Philadelphia family, but very simple, very nice people," she assured me. This portrait, too, caused its own drama. After Ella died in 1999, I learned in a letter from Wetherill's son, Francis D. Wetherill, that "the painting was done in return for some legal services." Characterizing himself as "an old man who is still angry at 82 years old," Francis wrote telling me, "Alas, the painting has been destroyed." He recalled a night in 1928: "In a party of too much revelry, one of my cousins after a few too many apparently decided she 'did not like the painting and did not want Laurie to be remembered that way.' What an outrage! She destroyed it. The next morning I was a very disappointed eleven-year-old boy. I loved my father *and* the painting."

Ella indicated a portrait she'd made of a twelve-year-old girl who lived in Spring City. "When her grandmother saw it," Ella told me, still clearly perturbed, "she asked me why I had painted her granddaughter without a smile." And I heard about the Spring City resident who wanted Ella to paint her husband. Ella had dismissed the idea, saying, "No, he's not interesting enough," most likely unaware that her usual directness would not be appreciated.

She eventually abandoned portraiture entirely and devoted herself to interpreting the infinitely less flawed, less socially encumbered land.

The sun was setting when I got back to the ranch house. Its isolation and proximity to Ella were just what I needed that summer. Sprawling on one hundred acres of grassy meadows surrounded by enormous pine trees, the house's interior revealed some of its owner's passions and preoccupations through his collection of Native American and Polynesian art, his leisure indicated by a well-used old saddle hanging in the bedroom.

Late the night I had arrived, before Dan left for a two-week trip, we'd gazed fifteen miles south through his antique sailor's telescope across the black night skies of Fairview, Mt. Pleasant, Spring City, and Ephraim to see the Manti Temple illuminated like a distant castle high on a hill, an otherworldly beacon shining in the dark valley.

Now I sat on the deck alone as the day concluded, feeling the warmth of the Utah summer still soft on my skin, watching the horses slowly grazing, the magpies squawking, their wings flashing blue iridescence while Dan's old dog dozed nearby.

I thought about all Ella had told me of her early American lineage—about one forefather who had built a small plot of East Coast land into a great holding, another who owned a fleet of ships that exported goods abroad, and another who established a mercantile business at the edge of the frontier to provide goods for the pioneers exploring westward. I thought about her late-eighteenth-century desk, conspicuously elegant in her simple home. I pictured the framed remnant of ancient Chinese embroidered silk resting on the mantle, its gold and red floss catching the soft light. All of it represented a heritage that provided the Germantown privilege Ella knew as a child.

I thought also about my own very different background during the quiet dusk of the ranch that summer, about my Armenian immigrant grandparents I knew so well, with their familiar broken English, their Old Country stories, and their jumble of children that created my aunts and uncles and cousins who remind me, still, who I am.

My grandfather, with a five-hundred-dollar fortune in his pocket, and my grandmother, his young bride arranged through their parents, crossed the Atlantic on an Italian steamer, leaving the Old Country at the end of 1912 and arriving in the United States in 1913. I can still hear my grandmother's voice as she told me in wonder about eating spaghetti for the first time on that ship. And, laughing at herself, she remembered rushing up from steerage expecting to see the fabled Statue of Liberty when she confused shipboard cries of "New Year" with "New York." But my grandmother and grandfather brought no Governor Winthrop desks or Sheraton gate-leg tables to hand down to their children. They had no leather-bound family histories or blue-willow plates, no ivory-handled silverware. Yet my black-and-white photograph of their wedding day, taken in the Old Country, captures that same determination and acceptance of circumstances that Ella's Dutch ancestors had carried with them to the New World centuries earlier.

That my father was a first-generation American seems no more remarkable to me than Ella's "blue-blooded" birthright seemed to her. Yet her privileged background held a mystique for me, especially because she was so clearly a product of it yet so evidently resistant to its elitist trappings.

My parents married in 1939—the same year Ella married Bill—in a small ceremony in my mother's home in Monterey Park, California. Their only wedding photo shows them standing in front of a fireplace, my mother wearing a dark knee-length dress and ankle-strap black heels, my father with a full head of dark wavy hair. As a child, I loved to open the carved Chinese trunk my mother kept in the dark of my brother's closet and take out that dress, just to feel the texture of the deep-green crepe fabric embroidered with seed pearls, to touch the surface of their youthful lives.

I treasure two photos symbolic of their hopeful early years: a snapshot of my father as a gymnast in college, standing perfectly built—tall, dark, and handsome—alongside the parallel bars, and another of my mother reclining on a lawn, strawberry blonde and laughing into the sunlight. These were people I never knew, and I only imagine the light green of their innocence.

I wondered that night about our tendency for categorizing experiences, for trying to make sense of our pasts. I began to realize that the stories I've told about the deckle-edged snapshots glued onto the black pages in my childhood photo album often become the memory, my renditions turned into the reality of my early years.

In working to find truth in my history, I was encumbered with my own unassailable perceptions. And in trying to find the truth of Ella's life, I was doubly burdened, first with her firmly set personal understandings reduced by her failing memory, and then by my own biased and often romanticized perspective of her stories.

That first summer after my divorce as I searched for meaning and new direction in Sanpete County, I began to pay more attention to the photos I was making of my own life's record, trying to distinguish between the portraits and the landscapes to understand both the particulars and the abstractions.

After spending mornings seeking out collectors of Ella's art throughout Sanpete County and afternoons talking with Ella, I returned to the ranch each evening. My need for solitude apparently boundless, I sat for hours on the big deck listening to the profound silence of the canyon going dark, comforted by nature's ever-changing constancy. I stared for hours at the night sky's offering—a cathedral domed with stars, clearly an amplitude of potential.

The next afternoon in her living room, Ella and I continued our perusal of her photo album, and I learned the source of her connection to nature as well as the foundation of her fierce resolve to live independently. I spotted a candid five-by-seven-inch photo of a good-looking young man standing on a beach, a long pier in the background.

"That's my father, holding some of us," Ella explained, reverence in her voice. Thick dark hair tousled on his forehead, her youthful and handsome father grinned into the camera, his muscular legs distributing the weight of the four children he held on his shoulders and in his arms. George Albert Smyth was at the family's summer home on the New Jersey shore in Lavallette when that photo was taken, most likely on one of his long weekend visits. "Father was my favorite person," Ella confided.

And as the hours passed, I came to understand through her stories of him how at odds his "sensitive and artistic nature" was with his place in Philadelphia society. George Smyth, pressured into attending law school by his parents, studied and practiced corporate law because, Ella pointed out, "he couldn't stand criminal law." She told me of her father's social conscience. He was a generous and kind man who did "a lot of free work" in addition to his corporate advocacy for Young, Smyth, Field Company, the family wholesale import and export business: "If people could pay, they paid. But if they couldn't pay, he still took care of them."

But the stress of practicing law overwhelmed him. He would come home exhausted after testifying in court and rest by lying supine on the hardwood floor, eventually suffering two nervous breakdowns, Ella reported, "from keeping the stress inside."

There was a rehearsed quality to her storytelling that day. Her childhood memories completely settled in her mind, she spoke in a practiced tone that would become familiar to me. Over the years of knowing Ella, I regularly prodded her to expand on her recollections, testing her for pliability, but it was seldom fruitful. And each year I visited her, she was less and less inclined to reflect on her past; apparently, I would have to be satisfied with the bare armature of anecdotes she offered.

I learned, during my subsequent summer visits, that whenever strangers, scholars, or friends asked Ella about the early influences on her life, usually wondering at the source of her determined independence, she would immediately speak of her father. Her response to that inquiry seemed simplistic, sounding especially routine in its delivery. Nearly every article about Ella quotes some version of his advice: "My father told all of us kids, 'Choose what you want to do in life and go after it. Don't think about how much money you'll make.'"

Now I can't help thinking his words meant more to Ella than a father's natural counsel and reassurance. I wonder if her repeated recitation of his advice disclosed a deeply ingrained defensiveness. In the face of a restrictive culture for women throughout the first seventy years of her life, she must have needed such support as she steadfastly eschewed women's customary occupations.

She must have kept her father's guidance in mind as justification for her unconventional attitude, clothing, and behavior; for her choice to study art instead of pursuing a more traditional education as a teacher; for her prolonged indifference to marriage; and eventually as defense of her career working as a draftsman to provide the main support for her own family.

She probably heard his words whispering in her ear when, as a young art student, she stubbornly rejected her family's social standing in Philadelphia society as she looked everywhere for ways to escape it literally and figuratively. Her father's pointed push to "go after" what she wanted drove Ella for a lifetime.

Ella had been openly exposing the source of the contradictions in her life that day. Though she wouldn't have articulated it, she had full comprehension of her own interior paradox—of her completely independent womanhood that clashed graphically with an essential uncertainty.

The difficulties she encountered as a young woman coming of age had left personal scars. And her sense of herself as an independent woman was always nudged by her struggle for that self-assertion within a male milieu—a place where patriarchal imperatives were a given and where women were well trained to follow them, a world that she, and other women like her, had to work hard to negotiate.

"You mentioned your family's beach house, Ella. Tell me more about it," I asked her. We were sitting on the theater chairs on her front porch. I wanted to know if she felt the way I did about the ocean, if she had the same respect for its power and splendor, found the same comfort in the sounds and rhythms of the surf.

"Lavallette was just a small town on the beachfront," she explained, "and I loved that. We really had a good time."

Ella's family, like many in the Germantown and Chestnut Hill sections of the city, escaped the heat of Philadelphia's summer to play at oceanside retreats. At first, Adelaide took her children south of Philadelphia to Sherwood on the Chesapeake Bay. Then, when Ella was five, they began renting in Lavallette, a small beachfront town on Long Beach Island on the New Jersey shore. Situated on a three-mile-wide peninsula, between Barnegat Bay and the Atlantic Ocean, Long Beach Island is an eighteen-mile-long stretch of towns strung along the main boulevard. After many summers of renting, the Smyths eventually bought a "cottage," actually a spacious two-story house with gray weathered shingled sides and large porches, an informal and modest contrast to the solidity and convention of their Germantown residence.

Her summers at the beach seemed to be Ella's only fond memories of childhood, "the good days," she called them, where her family relaxed their proper Philadelphia manners. She played for hours free of any authority, fishing, sailing, and bodysurfing. "After a northeast storm, we'd ride the breakers," she told me. "You'd have to relax. If you straightened up, you hurt your neck. You absolutely relaxed and you didn't get hurt at all."

When she was nine years old, her mother instructed her older sister, Mary, to teach Ella to sail and "was horrified to find out I'd been sailing for years!" She remembered sailing the family's sneak box and deliberately jumping overboard if she had stayed out too long, letting her mother think she was late returning home because the boat had capsized.

"Eller," as her sisters called her, learned practical skills from the chores demanded of the whole family each summer as they repaired the winter damage to the house. The children cleaned the fish they ate, scraped and painted their sailboats each summer, and repainted the beach house when the salt air damaged it. They hand-pumped water for the kitchen and bathtub in their early days there and used the toilet in their "White House" in the backyard.

Nights when the house was too full of guests, the Smyth children would sleep outside on the sand dunes, the rhythmic breaking of the waves their lullaby.

The clean, salty breezes, the freedom of being in the water, and the dropping of all pretenses allowed Ella to be comfortable in her own skin.

It was my last day in Spring City that summer, and Ella and I had spent the day meandering through her summer memories. She rummaged in the cupboard next to her fireplace looking for something she wanted to show me. It was a leather-bound program from her father's memorial service. Before I opened it, she started relating a seventy-five-year-old memory as though it had just happened.

"I was just thirteen years old when he was killed," she told me with the injustice of her loss quaking in her voice, "but I remember him so well. One Saturday Father was asked by his brother Calvin to drive him up the coast to help Uncle Calvin's son Billy, who was having car trouble. Father told Mother that he didn't want to go, but of course he went. On the way, a train hit Father's car at a crossing. My uncle was not hurt, but Father, just forty-six years old, was pinned, and the Ford caught fire. He died from burns in the hospital later that day."

Ella lost her "favorite person" that August in 1919, the one who had exerted the strongest influence on her life and who would permeate her thoughts until she died in 1999. It was Uncle Calvin who found a pincushion Ella had made for her father as a young girl in his pocket at the scene of the accident.

I opened the leather folder and read the text aloud. His colleagues honored George Albert Smyth as a "wise counselor, a gentleman and friend." The document acknowledged his "devotion to whatever was right and true."

"When Father died, it changed me," Ella said, with characteristic understatement. In fact, his death bereaved Ella of a soul mate, marked her countenance, and diminished her already fragile self-confidence, an effect easily seen in photographs from her adolescence, mostly showing an awkwardly tall young woman standing alone or apart from others in unsmiling anguish. On the cusp of adolescence she had abruptly lost the closest and strongest male influence on her developing young life.

But George Albert Smyth left his family well cared for financially, with most of their money in the family business. Hence, for two years, 1919 and 1920, Ella continued at the Germantown Friends School, and then entered Springside School, a prestigious private high school for girls established in 1879 in Chestnut Hill, near Philadelphia.

In 1920, however, the family business, with more than a million dollars in assets, most "tied up in goods exported to South America," went into receivership. "The U.S. government said South America would not have to pay their debts," Ella claimed. Thus, Young, Smyth, Field Company went bankrupt. "If Father had been there, he could have prevented it. This wiped out about three-fourths of my mother's money."

After her husband's death, "when the skies fell," according to her autobiography, Adelaide Smyth struggled to be both parents to five children—the youngest, Martha Jane, just eighteen months old. Ella remembered her mother attempting to make up for her husband's absence by "doing too much" for her children, "trying to make up to my two younger sisters for not having a father. I think they were quite spoiled. I felt that she did not love me much, but I am sure that was only in my mind. I think I was not much help to her."

Adelaide worked hard to provide "the best possible education Father always wanted each of us to have," Ella explained, but she ultimately had to sell off the family stockholdings, sell their summer cottage in Lavallette, and remodel the family home in Germantown into small rental apartments.

The second-most painful experience for Ella, after losing her father's close companionship, was being forced to attend public schools, "not very good places in Philadelphia in those days."

The administrators at Springside School wanted Ella to stay longer without paying tuition; her mother, however, refused to accept their "charity," and Ella didn't get to finish her Quaker education. From the fall of 1921 until December 1922, Ella attended the public Germantown High School, which she readily admitted she "couldn't stand." She recalled that public schools had "an awful reputation" at the time, with an atmosphere so "absolutely different" from the Friends School. "I dreaded it. There was lots of cheating; the students cheated using 'ponies.' I'd had three years of Latin and six years of French at that time but couldn't keep up. They would hide the translation in their books, so they could read it while they stood up to translate. The teacher had to know that. There were great big classes, and I couldn't take it in. They called the teachers by their first names. In the Quaker school the classes were much smaller, and the teachers were respected.

"I was amazed coming from a Quaker school and listening to some of the conversations going on among the girls. They talked about everything amazing about boys, and they were very outspoken, and I wasn't used to that. It was just too much for me. It was frivolous. All I did was worry the whole time.

"I was supposed to stay there for lunch, and we didn't even have an hour for lunch. We lived one and a half blocks from the high school, and I used to run home at lunchtime so I wouldn't have to stay at school to eat. So I was a very bad girl and left at Christmas of my senior year because I was fed up. So I'm a dropout!"

Ella's brother, Albert, was forced to leave school to work. He started a small company selling women's foundation garments, goods left from the family's ill-fated business. Ella worked in that shop the remainder of her senior year.

We'd been sitting on her sofa for hours, both of us moved by her childhood transition from seaside freedom to loss and privation. "Come in here; I want to show you something," Ella said. I followed her into her bedroom, past her fine old cherry-wood four-poster marriage bed, to examine a framed photograph on the wall.

Here was Ella at sixteen, her long hair spread loosely on her shoulders, wearing an embroidered white organdy dress and the solemn expression of a daughter still grieving her "favorite person." "That was my dancing-school dress, and those are the amber beads Father brought me from Bermuda. He always wrote letters to me when he was away. He must have known when I really needed his help and guidance."

◈ ◈ ◈

I drove home the long way that June, down through Utah's Dixie to Southern California, planning to see my parents for a few weeks before I headed north for home. Stopping only for gasoline and a cold drink, I seemed to fly across the silence of the scattered towns and dramatic rock forms of the southern Utah desert. Then, too soon it seemed, I was beyond the Las Vegas city limits where billboard after billboard advertised fast food and discount malls in Barstow.

When I reached the coast and my parents' home, the pastel colors of late-afternoon light flickered on the darkening sea. I sat a while on the still-warm sand of the deserted beach and listened to the waves pounding and the shorebirds screeching.

I had spent much of my childhood and adolescence at Southern California beaches. I prize my memories of two weeks every summer spent with my cousin on the Balboa Peninsula, bonfires at Huntington Beach with our neighbors, and riding paddleboards on Newport Bay during our stays in tiny cottages on Balboa Island. The beach is still an easy refuge for me. Without any challenge at all, I can spend hours staring at the waves and breathing the Pacific's healing air.

Watching the breakers late that afternoon, I kept thinking about Ella's offhand remark while we were out "looking" the week before. She had mused nearly to herself as she stared out the car window at the venerable land, "The desert throws back to the seashore a lot." And it's true that the desert is a prehistoric seabed.

I reflected on the paradox of this woman who had come into her own as a child by the sea finding her spiritual home in a small town set in the vast Great Basin of the Utah desert. That vista of desert silt and sand that had moved so effortlessly beneath an ancient ocean now stretched invitingly before her, rich with possibility.

Ella engaged resolutely with the apparent world—feeling the sandy soil under her nails as she dug up sagebrush, scratching her worn fingers on a coarse cow's skull she picked up in the western hills of Sanpete County, and ripping her pant leg climbing through barbed wire with her dog, Jeffery, to find the perfect spot to paint vertical red-rock cliffs outside Springdale. She hunted down the harsh reality of Mary Austin's "land of little rain," seeking out barren earth blanketed white with snow in winter and parched golden in summer. She communed best with a land dominated by a ragged and degraded "trash plant"—the big sagebrush, vegetation recurrently destroyed by wildfires.

I lay in bed each night that week listening to the surf's pounding rhythms and wondered at Ella's strength.

The Girl in the Red Scarf. OIL, 24″ x 36″. COURTESY OF BRIGHAM YOUNG UNIVERSITY MUSEUM OF ART.

The Girl in the Red Scarf

You were made and set here to give voice to this,
your own astonishment.
—Annie Dillard, *The Writing Life*

T HE BUS LET ME OUT across the street from the National Museum of Women in the Arts, a massive stone building and restored former Masonic temple in a busy part of Washington, D.C., a few blocks from the White House. The bus driver had pointed to it, a good thing because I couldn't see its sign; at first glance I couldn't even distinguish it from the other buildings alongside it.

I was in Washington that October visiting my friend Helen for a few days before I took the train north to Philadelphia and Manhattan, then to upstate New York. Because I had taken a year's leave, an unpaid sabbatical of sorts, I experienced the rare treat of traveling in the fall, the best part of the year on the East Coast. It was perfect weather in Washington that day, still warm and without much humidity.

When Helen left to teach her classes my last day there, I walked a few blocks from her 1860s brick town house to Union Station, its own wonder of restoration, to catch the city bus to this museum I'd first read about in my guidebook the night before.

Then I walked into the museum's magnificent interior—all spaciousness and hushed cool marble—to see its serious dedication to women's art. I wandered for a while around the galleries on the bottom floor, looking at paintings and sculpture that told women's wide-ranging stories, then climbed the graceful stairs that curved halfway around the foyer, drawn to an exhibit of artists' books in the third floor's Library and Research Center.

After an hour among the diverse, funny, poignant, and simply beautiful expressions of womanhood arrayed in display cases in the library, I wandered the stacks looking for information about the Philadelphia School of Design for Women (PSDW) that Ella attended in the early 1920s. I found it in Nina Walls's recently published University of Delaware dissertation, *Art, Industry, and Women's Education: The Philadelphia School of Design for Women, 1848-1932*. Walls described the school's history and its pointed mission in the beginning of the 1900s: to provide training in practical skills critical for the advancement of Philadelphia's growing design industry. Yet in the 1920s the school also taught fine arts—landscape painting, figure drawing, and sculpture.

That morning, my "Ella Project," as I'd come to call it, seemed to take on import I hadn't previously considered. I'd been conducting somewhat random research for the past few summers, talking to anyone associated with Utah art, spending hours with Ella, reading about the desert—all without clear purpose, without any form of a final product in mind.

Unexpectedly, upstairs in the library of the National Museum of Women in the Arts, I became conscious of a depth and wholeness of context to Ella's life story. In the few hours I spent scanning Walls's dissertation before leaving to meet Helen for lunch, I got my first glimpse of the source of what I would come to admire as Ella's art ethic—hard work for art's own sake, driven by an impulse to create and connect with the world.

That morning I appreciated for the first time the value that art school must have had to Ella—offering her a foundation in both the practicality and the aesthetic of art. She had found a purpose so freeing and energizing it motivated deep devotion to her "own astonishment" at the world around her for the rest of her life.

I left Washington, D.C., by train early the next morning to be on time for an afternoon appointment at Ella's art school in Philadelphia. The taxi let me out in front of the Moore College of Art and Design, the renamed and relocated Philadelphia School of Design for Women now situated a few miles from the Philadelphia Museum of Art.

I stood outside in the bright light of that fall day for a few minutes to absorb the view. The school's modest glass and aluminum-fronted building faced the Benjamin

Franklin Parkway at Logan Circle, one of the five original city squares of Philadelphia. Cars and buses sped along the roadway between the college and the spacious Swann Memorial Fountain.

Still "small and urban" with merely five hundred students, the Moore College of Art and Design remains "the only degree-granting women's art college in the country and one of two in the world," according to a brochure I picked up as I entered. Upstairs, above the foyer and gallery, the librarian, Sophia Herwyk, loaded me up with books that documented the school's history, graduation programs from 1924 to 1927, and several boxes of old photographs.

The school had originated in 1848 with drawing classes in the home of Sarah Worthington Peter, a prominent Philadelphia philanthropist who, with a group of Quaker friends, set out to help "deserving women. . .on the edge of privation and suffering" become self-supporting. The school's original purpose was focused on women's needs to support themselves and "flourish in a world that still denies them their full due." Years after its founding, an article in a 1932 issue of *Art Digest* characterized the PSDW as a destination for women only after they had had "their chance at orange blossoms," apparently suggesting that studying art served as a consolation prize for old maids.[5]

By the time Ella Gillmer Smyth entered the school in 1924, Sarah Peter's mission to provide "training for women that could lead to careers and financial independence" was highly organized and effective. The school regularly contracted with East Coast manufacturers to design textiles, floor coverings, upholstery fabric, wallpaper, book illustrations, and wood engravings to counter a U.S. dependence on European imports.

As I read on, my mind widened to a greater understanding of Ella's early life: her own edge of privation, her need to support herself, the practical art she made for forty-three years following art school, the thought of orange blossoms far from her mind—all of it anticipated in Sarah Peter's progressive goals determined forty years before Ella was born.

The stacks of vintage black-and-white photographs from the 1920s showed formally clad women standing in front of tall stools that held small clay statues they were sculpting from a model, women gathered for a masked ball in front of wall murals Ella later told me she had helped paint, brick buildings on a quad laced with paths that Ella reported she had hurried down—once again losing track of time painting outdoors and finding herself late for her life-drawing class.

Almost as an afterthought, Sophia handed me the January–February 1998 issue of *American Art Review* with an article, "The Philadelphia Ten: A Women's Artist Group," describing a group who exhibited from 1917 to 1945.[6] I opened the magazine to see pages of paintings evocative of Ella's style—impressionistic renderings of East Coast landscapes in the same muted tones of Ella's palette, large sedate portraits, and, notably, a vast landscape of the western desert painted by Mary-Russell Ferrell Colton, later a noted Arizona regional artist.

The article told of the Philadelphia Ten artists, several associated with the PSDW, who exhibited annually during the years Ella was married and not painting. Described as an "all-women's American regional artist group that exhibited longer and more widely than any other," the original group included Ella's good friends from art school, women older than she—Arrah Lee Gaul, a drawing instructor, and Constance Cochrane, a lecturer on history and appreciation of art at the PSDW during Ella's years there.[7] The article described the gold-leafed frames Cochrane's mother had made for her, reminding me of some of Ella's stories of learning to carve and burnish frames to help support herself after art school.

The Philadelphia School of Design for Women directly and indirectly taught Ella the single-minded ideals of the Arts and Crafts movement—a practical way of seeing art as it evolves from nature, organically and with little ornamentation. Originally an outgrowth of a resistance to industrialization in England at the turn of the century, the movement eventually became seen as uniquely American. The Arts and Crafts ideals are centered in nature and natural expression. They focus on a desire to make meaning in the world through mindfulness in art and daily living.

It was during art school that Ella learned to use carving tools to build and carve the moldings for her own frames. It was then she learned the printmaking techniques she would later employ for years to make her annual Christmas cards in Spring City. Most critically, it was in art school that she learned to respond directly to the land, to avoid the artifice that can result from painting landscape from a photograph. And it was during art school and afterward that she learned the work ethic that encouraged a complete connection to the subject and product of her industry.

Finally, her knowledge of the craftsmanship intrinsic in the Arts and Crafts movement equipped her with both a desire and an ability to discover her own fit into the western land, a place she eventually documented with wonder.

On the train heading for New York City's Penn Station late that afternoon, I imagined the marvelous discovery art school must have been for Ella and anticipated hearing her stories of those years.

The next summer Joe and Lee Bennion offered me their Spring City home to work in for a few weeks in August in exchange for doing some chores while they rafted the Colorado River. I planned to sleep in the house and feed the horses and dog while I spent as much time with Ella as I could.

Spring City had become comfortable to me; I felt myself more settled there, its clean air, clear blue skies, and spaciousness seeming to slow down my mind's chatter. Feeding the horses was a challenging and vigorous diversion. I enjoyed it all: the horses' big, sweaty bodies, the worn pitchfork I stabbed into the dusty hay, the cats' attitude of propriety as they nonchalantly supervised my task.

Spring City also attracted me because so many accomplished artists worked and lived there, many whose work was recognized outside Utah. That summer I hoped to understand Ella's place in this informal and, at that time, relatively obscure art colony.

My admiration for the Bennions had grown over the years. Working artists, parents, and active members of their community and church, they made their living through their art—simply and directly, Joe with his pottery and Lee with her painting.

I always warmed to the worn but clearly honest style that permeated the Bennions' home, as well as to the starkness of their choice and the clarity of their dedication to practicing Mormonism, albeit as independently as possible. They were the kind of Mormons I felt relaxed with, the sort of people who didn't feel uncomfortable around anyone who might deviate from the church's narrow guidelines.

The Bennions became early friends of Ella and Bill's when the Peacocks moved to Spring City. Early on, Lee worked alongside Ella in a summer workshop, and Joe had encouraged Ella's first showing of her art in Utah.

The Bennions' brick "pattern-book farmhouse" with adobe interior walls became their home in 1977 when both of them were still commuting to Brigham Young University in Provo, Utah, to finish their degrees in art. Their two-story corner house just a few blocks from Ella's sits on a quarter-block lot with a large barn and horse corral, an underground Native American sweat lodge Joe uses, and a nineteenth-century log cabin they restored for Lee's studio.

I came down from Salt Lake a few days before they left to learn what they needed me to do. That morning I knocked and then walked in the front door that opens directly to the Bennions' large, very lived-in dining room centered by an old round oak table surrounded by antique chairs. A coal stove covered in memorabilia, mail, and other necessities sat cold that summer day, awaiting its primary job of radiating heat throughout the downstairs in winter.

Two walls, lined with shallow shelves holding all manner of Joe's pottery—cups, bowls, plates, tea bowls, and honey jars—face two other walls filled, salon-style, with paintings. Some are Lee's images depicting her family—Louisa as a child contemplating her reflection in a hand mirror, Joe's sister standing in front of a window holding a long-stemmed lily, a small, stylized landscape of the Grand Canyon.

Ella's paintings were there, too—*Being Demolished, Manti Temple in Winter,* and her first depiction of the Lehi Roller Mills. Hanging above a sideboard, a conspicuous sign provoking its readers to "Challenge Authority" caught my eye every time I walked in.

I walked through the kitchen past several clay pots full of red geraniums blooming opulently beside the stove and in every windowsill—flowers that frequently populated Lee's paintings—to the back porch steps, across the yard, past the clothesline and expansive garden, to reach Lee's studio where she had told me she might be working to complete some paintings promised to her agent.

Inside Lee's studio, I settled on a pressed-back oak side chair next to a small claw-footed bathtub she had installed in a corner. Tall, with long straight dark-blonde hair that reached her hips, Lee reflected a study in practical directness. She was painting on a large canvas, depicting a tall, thin woman—not unlike herself—wearing a straw hat and holding enormous stalks of red and green rhubarb. Lee works in rich-hued oils on canvas, usually painting female figures in familial settings, occasionally landscapes. She evokes spiritual moods in her stylized compositions that are often accented with objects and imagery of personal significance—a bird's nest, a feather, a sliver of a moon.

Like nearly everyone I met who collected Ella's paintings or who knew Ella, Lee responded eagerly to my questions, sharing, with a firm respect, her story of meeting Ella the summer the Bennions moved to Spring City when both women attended an outdoor painting workshop at Snow College's Summer Snow Program.

Lee soon learned that she didn't like working on location, that her landscape painting required more contemplation than plein air painting permitted: "My landscapes are more of a synthesis of what I've seen and thought and felt over time; it comes through me," she explained. "Ella paints a direct response to what she's seeing, and for me that would be harder to do. She really captures a lot of soul and feeling. Many artists who work that way don't, but I think she does."

We talked about Ella's persistence at painting outside in all kinds of weather, at her insistence on staying inside her car to work.

Lee smiled and said, "Ella paints in her car all year long. Her old Toyota station wagon was charming inside, covered with little dabs of paint all over the dash, the steering wheel, and the ceiling. She doesn't like to sit outside the car because people stop and bug her, but, on the other hand, when she's sitting there in her car people who drive by stop and ask if she's all right.

"But Ella's and my work are very different. Two or three times a year, people say they can tell our work is similar. We laugh about it. I think it's because we're both women and we both live in Spring City—and because of the frames."

More likely, I thought, it's because both women are tall, lean, and independent artists who disregard most conventions in their appearance and their art. They both prefer long periods of solitude and eschew the superficial socializing popular in most small towns.

And then there *are* the frames. The women's subject matter and styles are completely dissimilar; however, both artists carve the molding for their own frames. Ella learned to carve her simple and unsophisticated frames of necessity in the 1920s then fifty years later taught Lee, who adapted the method to make it her own. Whereas Ella's frames are coarsely carved and subtly tinted with washes that evoke her tonalist palette, Lee's highly colored, more refined carving reflects the same careful attention to shape and color she creates in her images.

The studio door opened and Joe joined us. As the three of us talked on while Lee painted, I relaxed into the ease of the Spring City style—at once both casual and purposeful. Joe was chattier than Lee, relishing odd bits of gossip and funny stories, eager to talk about the curiosities underlying their lives.

Joe recalled Ella's first exhibit in Utah. He was showing his pottery at the Wilkinson Gallery at Brigham Young University in December 1978. "I wanted some paintings on the walls to complement my pots," he said. "So I approached Ella. She had been painting here in Spring City for nearly ten years before that. She had a lot of work stacked up all over her house, and she hadn't even thought about exhibiting it or doing anything with it."

Joe laughed about the materials Ella had used—"really common materials." She was painting on dam canvas she bought at the feed company, canvas that farmers used to make dams for their ditches. And she would go to the dump and salvage wood to make stretcher bars. "But," Joe insisted, "she was really particular about wood that she carved for her frames and bought sugar pine from a mill in Salt Lake."

We talked about an artist's life, the near poverty Joe and Lee chose when they first moved to Spring City where they eventually raised three daughters, the odd jobs they held as each of them took turns driving to Provo to finish art school while the other cared for their growing family.

I saw the Bennions' lifestyle in Spring City as a realization of Ella's art ethic—that ability to render most concerns secondary to the need to create while living mindfully and purposefully on the land. Their values and practices provide a model of nineteenth-century industry fitted thoughtfully into the twenty-first century. Significantly, they manage the tension generated by the parallel callings of duty and art.

◆ ◆ ◆

I looked forward that summer to learning more about Ella's artistic inspiration and her experience becoming an artist. Most of all, I wanted to listen closely enough to hear her tell me what made her, in her eighties, so determined to keep at it. After all, here was a woman many would call elderly whose days were completely occupied with her art, a woman who wasn't languishing into her old age playing cards with the local widows. Instead, she seemed to be at full attention in the moment, a quality hardly nurtured by the contemporary American zeitgeist. She contributed meaningfully, searching daily for old and new stories to authenticate artfully in that quietly powerful place.

"What do you suppose inspired you to become an artist when you were a child?" I asked Ella. She couldn't really answer me. She said she "just knew" that's what she wanted to do after she left high school. Again I felt frustrated in my attempts to go beyond surface anecdotes, behind the familiar answers she had practically memorized. She was also discouraged with her sketchy responses. "I think I'm about finished here, over the hill," she told me that day.

I told her about *Voyage to Windward,* the J. C. Furnas biography of Robert Louis Stevenson I was reading at the time. Furnas talked about Stevenson's first realization of his future as a writer and said that all artists and writers have a time in their childhood when they recognize the beauty in common things and are touched.

I asked if she'd had such experiences. "Oh, yes, sure," she answered quickly. "We spent our summers at the beach, and I used to sit in the sand dunes and watch the storms come in over the ocean. It made me see things."

I smiled thinking of the child Ella had been, her mind already forming around that private perception of the world that sets artists apart from their peers.

"Listen, I painted those in art school," Ella said suddenly, indicating the art I'd long admired, two large-scale portraits, each approximately twenty-four by thirty-six inches, hanging in her living room—*The Girl in the Red Scarf* and *Honey Ross*—dear keepsakes that graced her living room even after they had been promised with the rest of a collection of her work to Brigham Young University. Both paintings showed the dignified character of calm women looking directly at the viewer, women whose figures filled the large canvases.

The Girl in the Red Scarf was especially rich with presence. A young woman with delicate arms and long, gentle fingers clasped in her lap gazes carefully with somewhat guarded brown eyes. Her red scarf contains her dark hair and is balanced by more red fabric in her skirt that meets the margin of the painting's foreground. Her classically styled white blouse fits loosely, draping gracefully.

It's the strength in the bearing of the women in *Honey Ross* and *The Girl in the Red Scarf* that distinguishes each of them as subjects respected for their womanhood, rather than the comely womanliness that a male painter might be more inclined to emphasize. It seemed to me that Ella could see the two qualities were one.

"And that's my death mask," Ella announced, bringing me out of my serious contemplation of the portraits, as she pointed to the clay remnant from her sculpture class staring vacant-eyed from her mantle, a bird feather stuck behind it. "My instructor in art school Sam Murray asked who wanted to volunteer, and I did. So he made my death mask to show us how."

"And I'll get my diploma to show you," Ella said, already on her way through her studio to her kitchen. She found it, buried deep in a pile of papers along with the deed to her house in a metal lockbox. The large, square diploma from the Philadelphia School of Design for Women, its border of gold flourishes now brittle and fading, attested, along with her death mask and the somber portraits of sturdy women, to her most valued accomplishments.

That week I thought a lot about Ella in the 1920s. I could easily imagine the independent woman she was in art school, full of inner drive and independent spirit. I better understood the resolutely misanthropic attitudes she had always defended, resisting other culturally imposed conceptions of womanhood.

Her androgynous appearance, for one thing, started during the 1920s: she had bobbed her hair, worn men's slacks and vests, and taken up smoking then. These were the years she began using her less feminine middle name, Gillmer, the name she would be identified by for the next forty-eight years until she moved to Utah. Her fellow art students called her Gillmer, and she was Aunt Gillmer to her nieces and nephews. She signed all her letters during these years solely with her middle name, or just Gill.

Essentially, she reinvented herself then, transforming from a rather sullen adolescent photographed in her "dancing-school dress" visibly mourning her lost father into a somewhat genderless young person who dared to defy convention. By declaring herself the epicene Gillmer, replacing conventional feminine clothing with masculine apparel, learning to drive a car as soon as legally allowed, she, perhaps, unmasked the person she was meant to be. Ella had successfully converted her childish temper tantrums of willfulness into a constructive determinacy.

But during the summers I visited her, during her late eighties and early nineties, I didn't always hear the confidence in her voice that this Gillmer must have had during the 1920s and 1930s. It seemed to me that she had been an organic feminist as a young woman, taking for granted her right to self-government, assuming the responsibility of providing for herself, making her own meaning. But now her voice frequently sounded apologetic and self-effacing. I could often hear the willfulness in her tone, but occasionally a weariness too, as though she found it difficult to continue stoking the fire of her independent being.

"Tell me about art school," I encouraged Ella that day. "Did you always know you wanted to study art?" Having come to appreciate Ella's impetuosity, I wasn't really surprised to learn that her artful life was more happenstance than plan. Because she had disliked high school and her academic confidence was so low, eighteen-year-old Ella didn't even consider attending a university after she suddenly left high school halfway through her senior year. Her mother encouraged her to study music, so she enrolled in music classes at the Peabody Conservatory in Baltimore where she lived for the fall semester of 1922 while her older sister, Mary, was studying mathematics at Goucher College on an academic scholarship.

Ella remembered riding her bike through the Goucher campus to meet Mary for Sunday breakfast. "I kept thinking how glad I was not to have to go to college," Ella told me. Typically integrating grit and self-doubt, she went on, "Mary thought college was the only thing to do if you had any brains at all. Maybe I should have been more like Mary. But I didn't *want* to be like her."

However, the study of music wasn't for Ella either: "I decided I didn't want to do that. I got to talking to another girl in my boardinghouse who was going to art school, and that just sounded to me like what I wanted to do. I just hoped I could do it."

Though the young Gillmer Smyth was choosing her future nearly incidentally, she was prepared, however unaware, with an incipient art ethic that included both strong work habits and eyes practiced at seeing. Still, Gillmer couldn't have managed the finances for art school tuition had it not been for her mother's good friend Bessie Ballinger. "Bessie was born and brought up in the ghost town of Silver City, Nevada, in a home dug out of the side of a hill," Ella recalled. Her wealthy husband, Walter Ballinger, was "a very fine architect in Philadelphia who was killed in a car wreck not too long after my father was. He left her plenty of this world's goods." But, Ella assured me, Ballinger "wasn't interested in a person's social standing or how much money they had, just the person."

Bessie Ballinger helped Adelaide Smyth finance the conversion of the Smyth family home into apartments and offered to help in other ways that Adelaide refused. However, Adelaide had what she called her "pride in scholarship," and readily accepted Ballinger's offer of a "private scholarship" for her unpredictable daughter.

Gillmer studied art at the Maryland Institute in Baltimore for one year beginning in the fall of 1923, taking the recommended classes in interior design and fashion design, and later called these classes "my least concerns."

In October 1924, Gillmer began her second year of study by enrolling in the Philadelphia School of Design for Women, the place where her art sensibility blossomed and flourished. Bessie Ballinger continued her private scholarship at the PSDW for another year, after which Gillmer earned the school's Senatorial Scholarship for her remaining years.

At the time, the Philadelphia School of Design was located at the corner of Broad and Master Streets in Philadelphia. Gillmer lived in the family home, by then converted into apartments, while she attended classes. She eventually used her developing carpentry skills to convert the attic into a studio—complete with a skylight—where she painted large portraits, including those that now hung in her living room.

The philosophy of art education at the PSDW was influenced by its founder's vision as well as by the legacy of the renowned American artist and steel engraver

John Sartain, who became president of the school in 1868. His daughter Emily and his granddaughter Harriet, who also led the school as principals, reinforced his vision of rigorous training for women.

Although the PSDW underwent many changes in leadership and overt philosophy throughout the years of its development and through seven changes in address, Sarah Peter's basic intention to focus on teaching women marketable skills endured. From its inception, the school's goals, in addition to teaching marketable skills, included creating an "image of genteel respectability and an atmosphere of conservative propriety" at the school. Emily Sartain, the principal from 1886 to 1918, suggested that the school educate "not only the producer but the consumer," implying that, upon leaving the school, the young women would consume as well as contribute to the market for expensive consumer goods, including paintings and sculpture.[8]

During the tenures of Emily and later her niece, Harriet Sartain, the directors of the PSDW prided themselves on remaining current with the best European art schools and with the nearby Pennsylvania Academy of the Fine Arts. Thus, Emily Sartain introduced French drawing techniques into the curriculum, methods that emphasized three-dimensional renderings rather than reproductions of plane surfaces.

Emily Sartain also promoted the idea that "life and nature are urged for study, not only in studio work . . . but, when weather permits, in outdoor work from landscape and from animals. These diversified subjects of study, changing in aspect with varying surroundings, enforce the truth that art consists in the relation of things to each other."[9]

In fact, in 1890, the school organized a life class for the study of the full-length nude figure, "offering young girls the unique advantage of pursuing this study under the guidance of one of their own sex," a bold move just four years after Thomas Eakins was forced to resign from the Pennsylvania Academy of the Fine Arts for removing a drape from an otherwise nude model in a life-drawing class.[10] Ella's attitude toward the naturalness of the study of the nude figure was thus informed by a perspective that would later be challenged when she moved to Utah and into what could be considered the most artistically conservative culture in the western landscape.

In 1923, the year before Gillmer Smyth entered the PSDW, the school hosted the exhibition of the National Association of Women Painters and Sculptors. However, this same year, and during a time when the country's social mores were in transition as well, the Sartains' seemingly progressive attitudes were rocked when their values of art education and decorum clashed.

Dean Harriet Sartain, a well-known stickler for propriety, felt her students' morality was challenged by an exhibit of the work of avant-garde artists such as Picasso and Gauguin presented by the Barnes Foundation, claiming it would be a "bad thing to put any such ideas before susceptible minds."[11]

Also typical of the dynamic times, in the early 1920s, many PSDW students objected to the prohibitions against "smoking, going hatless out of doors and leaving the building without express permission." Dean Sartain "responded to [this] perceived lack of 'discipline' in the school with a newly formulated set of regulations" regarding the rigors of the curriculum, thus attempting to fortify her stand against the inroads of modern thinking.[12]

As we talked that day in Ella's living room and as I heard Ella's voice warm with passion, I began to hear the voice of the young woman called Gillmer who had finally found a sense of belonging in her twenties. "I loved art school," Ella told me. "I couldn't wait for Monday to come, couldn't wait for the weekend to be over.

"It was a better school, ahead of its times, I think," Ella claimed. "You didn't go into life classes until the third year, and then life class was all week—portrait, figure studies, and action. The biggest part of the day you learned to draw: superficial anatomy, bones and muscles."

Zealous to convert me, Ella wanted me to understand the distinctions between good and inferior art education. She explained the differences between the systems of instruction at both the Maryland Institute and the Philadelphia School of Design for Women, emphasizing the value of the traditional experience at the PSDW. She disapproved of the system at the Maryland Institute, where the instructors were professional teachers and the course work was, according to Ella, "a trial" of diverse classes, not driven by awareness of a logical scope or sequence.

Her instructors at the PSDW, in contrast, didn't "teach" art. Instead, they were all working artists whose professional practice was set aside twice a week to critique the young women's work; thus, their assessments, Ella felt, were informed honestly. The course work at the Philadelphia school was offered in a logical and strict sequence, requiring the basics of color theory, composition, anatomy, and drawing before allowing students to begin painting.

Late in life, Ella still disapproved of most public art education, citing her instructor George Harding, who told his students, "The way to cure any child from wanting to become an artist would be to have him take art in a public school. The less you know about the history of art until you are at least forty years old, the better off you are."

Ella insisted, "Children don't need instruction about how to put things down on paper. All they need to do is learn how to look and see, then put their own stuff down, whatever it is, whatever they see. But the important thing is just teaching them to see things. The more you do it, the more you see. I feel strongly about that. We never studied technique. Never. We would get criticisms, but nobody taught us how to paint. They wouldn't dream of that."

We leafed through graduation programs and catalogs I'd copied in the library at the Moore College of Art and Design. The illustrations accompanying each major field of study and the biographies of the faculty prompted Ella's memories and strong feelings about the value of finding one's own way under the guidance of demanding mentors.

She told me of the work she did for George Harding, who taught her illustration class. She helped in his efforts to paint murals for the Philadelphia Sesquicentennial Exhibition and for the seventy-fifth anniversary of the Hotel Pere Marquette in Peoria, Illinois, both in 1926. R. Sloan Bredin, a member of the New Hope group of painters, had taught life class—figure and portrait—and earned her respect. "It took most of every day, but we learned to draw," she remembered. Henry B. Snell, a Royal Academician and accomplished landscape painter, criticized the students' still-life and landscape work one day a week. Ella told me these "had to be done on the spot, on location. Your name would be mud if you painted from a photo."

Although the young women made sculptures, drawings, and still-life paintings in the school's studios, they worked unaccompanied to interpret the landscape. The opportunity to work alone painting on-site or making drawings for her printmaking, apart from the others' chatter and away from the strict eye of Harriet Sartain, must have heartened the rebellious Gillmer's sense of self and encouraged her penchant for solitude. She must have eagerly carted her drawing supplies to the wharf and sat for hours in the bracing air contentedly sketching the busy harbor. The eighteenth-century Philadelphia neighborhoods attracted her as well—the pattern and textures of brick buildings built right up to the narrow cobblestone streets.

Ella remembered most fondly Samuel Murray, her instructor in modeling from life, "a friend of Thomas Eakins." Murray was actually more than just a friend of Eakins. As a prolific sculptor during and after his association with the PSDW, he worked with Eakins for years, first as his student, later as his studio assistant. Eakins's excellent portrait of Murray's youthful beauty, to be sure, wasn't one of those portraits that offended the subject and for which Eakins was notorious.

But Ella remembers Murray most vividly because he championed her at a critical time. "Sam Murray chose me to receive the sculpture prize on my graduation, but Dean Harriet Sartain did not like or approve of me, so he refused to award one that year if he couldn't give it to me. Harriet Sartain finally gave in, and I got the award. So I'm sure that if, by chance, I was going to get the European scholarship, she would have put her foot down and it would have stayed down."

I opened the book *Design for Women: A History of the Moore College of Art* that I had picked up in Philadelphia, and Ella immediately pointed to Harriet Sartain's photograph. A slender woman with white hair pulled back, posing with a fountain pen in one hand, she sat at a desk, ostensibly checking attendance records. She wore a fair amount of artful jewelry and a scarf, and appeared to be a dignified elderly woman, not quite the formidable presence Ella had described. But Ella's deprecatory attitude toward the stern and officious Dean Sartain was unassailable and contrasted pointedly with the fondness she felt for her instructors.

Gillmer entered the Philadelphia School of Design for Women just after Dean Sartain had eased her "ridiculous rules," such as requiring the young women to wear hats out-of-doors. But she still monitored attendance personally and required the young women to get permission to leave the building and sign in when they returned. Miss Sartain allowed no visitors during school hours and no use of the telephone except during lunch and after classes.[13]

Despite her softening of previous stricter practices concerning life-drawing class, Harriet Sartain's beliefs in "nineteenth-century codes of gentility" clashed with Gillmer's cavalier attitude toward the school rules.

Ella told me, "Dean Sartain didn't like me because I would just forget things, and maybe I wasn't polite enough and thoughtful enough of the things I should do. Sometimes I wouldn't want to paint still life in the afternoon, so I'd just leave and go paint landscape and forget to sign out. Boy, was I in trouble with Dean Sartain for that!"

Gillmer's great admiration for her male instructors extended as well to many women faculty members, among whom she observed an independence of spirit and camaraderie. Her good friends were two older women instructors at the PSDW—Paula Balano, who taught charcoal and antique, and Constance Cochrane, a lecturer on history and art appreciation. "Miss Balano was the first woman to win the European scholarship when she graduated in 1900. She was quite a lady, loved to kid people. Told me at art school I drew like Holbein and painted like Velázquez—tongue in cheek!"

Her closest friend was fellow student Frances "Monty" Watson, an accomplished animal artist and a woman, according to Ella, "who could do nearly anything a man could do." Monty and Gillmer got on well in art school and remained partners in many endeavors throughout the following fifteen years and friends for many more.

As we sat on her sofa that afternoon, I looked around her living room and studio. Except for a few small prints and two watercolors by Paula Balano, all the art was Ella's. And all of it portrayed the same sensibility as the portraits and landscape paintings reproduced in the PSDW graduation programs from the years she attended, 1924-27—as though Ella had discovered herself during those years in art school and kept that discovery intact and unexpressed for nearly fifty years until she could rearticulate it in the West.

When she finally returned to painting in the late 1960s, Ella's style and painting technique had barely changed since art school—unlike Alice Neel, her famous classmate who had graduated two years earlier than Gillmer and whose style evolved from the conservative study of sedate figures painted in art school to expressionist Schiele-like portraits of bluntly realistic bodies.

Instead, Ella painted completely unaffected by modernism, her work in 1987 nearly replicating her 1927 style. This isn't to say she didn't grow as an artist, though she missed long years of such an opportunity; instead, she clung fast to her first impression of the world through paint.

The Arts and Crafts ideal of creating harmony in all life's aspects that Gillmer garnered in art school permeated her world. She completely lived the rule of nature coined by the nineteenth-century architect Louis Sullivan as the aphorism "form ever follows function." Gillmer was a young woman who learned in her formative years that golden mean of art. More important for me, she grasped something many women never experience: the opportunity to realize her passion.

After spending so much time that day immersed in Ella's art, I sat outside on the grass in the Bennions' front yard to watch the daylight turn into the gloaming, my favorite time of day. As an enormous moon filled the sky, I recalled a day in my childhood I'd nearly forgotten, the day I discovered my mother's artistic talent.

I'd already known she was creative. She designed and sewed all my clothes until I was thirteen, as well as an elaborate wardrobe for my blonde doll Sweet Sue, and she knit all my sweaters. I must have thought all mothers did those things. When I was twelve, I learned more.

One day while rummaging in a cupboard above my bedroom closet, I discovered my mother's 1930s high school art portfolio, newsprint brimming with appealing Arts and Crafts–style drawings of houses and trees, along with sheets of lined paper filled with lettering exercises, expertly rendered in an appealing font I'd never seen. Bewildered by this apparent evidence of her abandoned—and, it seemed to me, concealed—talent, I quickly returned the papers to their place in the closet, feeling guilty, as though I'd stumbled on my mother's secret identity. Likewise, I tucked away into my worldview the model of hidden potential this discovery provided, unconsciously placing it into my growing, and conflicting, definition of a woman's hapless purpose.

When my father retired and my parents moved to the coast south of Los Angeles, I encouraged my mother to take some art classes in their town of Laguna Beach, which had been an art colony in the 1920s, the same years Ella was in art school in Philadelphia. But my mother had become a different person by then and preferred weekly bridge parties and golf outings with her friends.

I realized that night that Ella's art initially appealed to me in part because of its resonance with my early connection to the Arts and Crafts sensibility. But it would be years before I truly appreciated the parallel between my mother and Ella and so many women of their generation who gave up pursuing their talents to meet societal and familial needs and expectations.

Ella was sixty-five years old before she fully embraced her identity, before she could leave the East and settle into her own element in the western desert. And it had taken many conscious acts of painting the desert's wildness again and again to cement that sense of self in place. Finally, that evening, I came to understand that I'd repeated the pattern as well: marrying young, I had completely lost track of myself during the ensuing twenty-five years.

In my reverie that night on the Bennions' lawn, I could still hear my grandmother's admiring words to me as a child. Holding me close to her silky dress, she often called me her "lucky girl." And, although I was never a particularly ambitious child or teen, I thought I *was* lucky, that if I really wanted anything, I could achieve it. Mostly what I wanted as a child was to replicate the model that my mother had set for me. And for many years, I had no regrets. I was satisfied with the challenge of rearing my children and creating a home for our family.

But that summer in Sanpete County, I could feel myself inexorably heading away from the person I'd been. Maybe I could sense the authority and clarity of this new direction that evening so vividly because Spring City was so nearly like another world to me. I was just far enough away from mine to begin to see where I'd been.

Out West. OIL, 24″ X 30″. COURTESY OF JACK AND KAREN BROTHERSON.

Out West

The desert is no lady.
She screams at the spring sky,
dances with her skirts high,
kicks sand, flings tumbleweeds,
digs her nails into all flesh.
Her unveiled lust fascinates the sun.
—Pat Mora, *The Desert Is No Lady*

IT WAS A CLEAR JUNE MORNING a year later, springlike and just starting to warm. Here and there, clumps of black-eyed Susans bloomed wildly along Highway 89, foregrounding the tawny landscape with bright contrast, as I once again drove from Salt Lake City to Sanpete County. This time I would stay in M'Lisa and Craig Paulsen's Spring City home, a carefully restored two-story stone Victorian. I found the hidden key where M'Lisa told me it would be, left my things in the kitchen, and walked over to Ella's, about five blocks away through the middle of town.

Most residents of Spring City, if asked about their favorite feature of the landscape, would point with pride to the expanse of the Wasatch Range, especially to Horseshoe Mountain that dominates the eastern horizon of Sanpete Valley. I've heard them speak with ardor of the canyons and the lush views from Skyline Drive. Most of them would characterize Sanpete County as farm country, but few would even mention that their town lies at the edge of the Great Basin of the western desert. The surrounding land—actually miles and miles of arid wilderness—exists in locals' minds as a kind of void, a mere backdrop to the preternaturally green perimeter of irrigated farmland.

That morning Ella and I drove toward the curving slopes of the western hills, both of us relaxing as soon as we were outside town, the car windows open to the warm air. We wound through the scattered farm communities of Chester, Moroni, and Fountain Green. Ella commented on nearly everything: the high price of gasoline, jarring new windows in an old house, a neglected barn. I laughed at her bold opinions.

As we drove along Highway 117, passing old stone houses and cemeteries, she said, "The desert has no business blossoming like a rose; that's all artificial. I don't want a lot of roses here; I would rather have sagebrush and desert flowers." I couldn't help smiling at Ella's mildly rebellious and proprietary attitude toward the desert. Preferring the unspoiled natural land, I had to agree. More and more lately, I noticed a similar stubborn and opinionated aspect in myself, a growing confidence in expressing my thoughts.

Every few minutes, she remarked on some detail of the desert landscape; sometimes she just stared out, turning her head suddenly at a curious cloud formation or a weathered sage branch. She wasn't interested in the small towns, except for their oldest buildings—usually a feed mill, a substantial brick bank, or an old pioneer-era adobe house. Mostly we both just basked in the warm air and open space between towns as we drove, enjoying the play of light on the desert and the pungent scent of the hardy, ever-present sage.

As we headed back to Spring City, she again regarded the farmland west of Spring City along Highway 89. "I'm not particularly interested in seeing all the nicely cared-for green fields. I like the desert, the way the country is naturally. Now there are more green fields here than there were, but you don't have to go too far to find the natural landscape. That's what's beautiful."

Ella had visualized herself as a westerner for nearly a lifetime before she settled in Spring City. Although movement westward to seek isolation, identity, and fortune was already a well-established American tradition, lore about western women probably impressed the young Ella as well. Wild West shows, begun by William Cody as Buffalo Bill in the 1880s, were still popular throughout the country when Ella was a child. She may have heard of Lucille Mulhall, America's first cowgirl, who had entertained in Madison Square Garden the year Ella was born.

Stories about her intrepid relative Georgie Short certainly fueled her childhood fantasies about the West. She told me, still marveling eighty years later, "Georgie helped finance Buffalo Bill's first Wild West show and collected the first night's profits—a barrel full of silver!" And when Ella was eleven, she learned that Calamity Jane's given name was Martha Jane, the same name as Ella's four-year-old sister. To her hopeful young mind this meant that she and Calamity Jane were related, and thereafter Ella pictured the wildness of the West as fundamental to her identity and inhabiting it as her personal destiny.

Her imagination must have helped her to some degree endure the stress of fitting in during her childhood and adolescence. In a photo showing her seated on a stone wall near her Germantown house, she looks awkward wearing a velvet skirt and a white blouse trimmed with metallic braid. Her despondency and discomfort mark her sixteen-year-old countenance, suggesting that the very act of dressing for the photograph must have been miserable for her. Here was a young woman confined in a proper and manicured hunter-green suburb of Philadelphia where, as she told me, "a girl's supposed to do what she's told," all the while harboring in her mind images of wide-open spaces shadowed in dusty pastels.

Perhaps, as she rode horses in Philadelphia in the correct English style, she pictured herself astride a stallion galloping in a desert, her hair flying behind her. When, at sixteen years old, she learned to drive, she probably reveled in the freedom a car afforded her to explore long distances under her own power.

Almost certainly, during high school and at the Philadelphia School of Design, young Gillmer viewed exhibits of the epic western imagery painted by Thomas Moran and Frederic Church, art that had for decades stirred the imaginations of many easterners about the West. Perhaps she "possessed some deficiency" that made her "subtly unadaptable to Eastern life," as Nick Carraway in *The Great Gatsby* sensed about himself.[14] At any rate, by the time Ella was twenty, she announced her liberation from meaningless boundaries by adopting the habits of rugged western men with their practical clothing, short haircuts, and great mobility.

Manifesting her own destiny, she drove westward across the country at least three times during the 1930s, always in the company of good women friends. Those trips fed her imagination and cemented her hope to leave the East for good.

◆◆◆

"I have a job!" Gillmer scrawled diagonally across the postcard she sent to her mother, who was vacationing in Lavallette with Gillmer's younger sisters. It was June 1927, a few weeks after her graduation from the Philadelphia School of Design for Women, and Ella was triumphant. She had been hired as a model for Martha Hovedon, "a fine sculptress I looked up to very much." Hovedon had a commission to create a life-size garden statue.

Ella relished telling me of her assignment: "I had to pose in the nude on my toes with my arms up in the air above me—standing next to a live deer! It was hard, but she let me rest when I had to."

After that first job, Ella was "fussing around with ways to make a living" and learned how to burnish gold leaf onto frames for her art. "One woman connected with the school of design taught me as a favor. I had asked all over how to do it, but it was a trade secret. This woman made frames for her daughter, who was an exhibiting artist I'd known in art school. There were fourteen processes to it. I still have the book with all the instructions."

She found a set of carving tools in a pawnshop for eighteen dollars, and during the years following art school she worked at home making frames and burnishing them for her own work and for an art shop in Philadelphia. "They paid me fifty dollars a frame and then sold it for one hundred. The carving came naturally to me."

Also at this time, Gillmer was invited to spend a year in Florence as a guest of "a family relative who married an Italian count." She remembered, "I was very busy with a so-called career then, and I should have been tied up and made to go. I could have furthered my education as well as seen the world." Still regretful sixty years later, she let her need to be financially independent—"to get after things" and support herself—take precedence over such an indulgence.

When the Great Depression challenged the country's mettle, Gillmer responded with spirit and ingenuity. All of her many jobs were art-related, but she painted comparatively little. She absolutely refused to apply for or accept any government assistance, believing she should take care of herself; thus, early on in her career, she established a lifetime principle of resisting and disapproving of aid to artists.

Though notable art of the period came from government-funded work, she especially disdained fellow artists who went to work for the Works Progress Administration (WPA). Ella told me, concerned that the WPA sounded too much like a government handout, "I wouldn't have been caught dead applying for a WPA job. I'm against that and don't want the country to get back to it. You can make it if you try hard enough."

In one of her most memorable stories of these difficult times, she recounted the embarrassing experience of her earnestness at piecework. She worked with a group of other women and alongside her close friend Monty Watson. The women painted flower designs on lamp shades for five cents a shade at a factory on the waterfront in Philadelphia.

"I wanted to make more money during that time, so I hurried up and worked faster. Because of me, they cut the rates down to four cents. So my name was mud!"

Working for "one of the best jewelers in Philadelphia, J. E. Caldwell Jewelers," Gillmer had the "murderous job" of designing new modern settings for beautiful old jewelry. "So lots of old settings just disappeared. It's a shame, isn't it?"

Three years after she graduated from art school, Gillmer went back to night school to complete a course in teacher education. Following that, she student-taught at her former high school, Springside School. She was required to follow a prescribed art curriculum, "carving bars of soap, drawing borders, and other such simplistic tasks—that's not art," she told me. She hated teaching, explaining, "I did work at it, but I was terrible; I couldn't do it. I felt sorry for the class."

While she was trying to make a living teaching art, Gillmer lived with Monty Watson and Monty's mother in an old stone house Monty was buying in Bucks County, Pennsylvania. "That's when I was put in jail for larceny and malicious destruction of property," she told me with more than a hint of satisfaction in her voice.

Monty's old house on an empty farm had been used as an illegal still during Prohibition. One weekend the women were busy improving the property—knocking down the old still and digging holes in the backyard for a water system. "We opened the garage to get a ladder, and while we were working someone stole a racing gig, one of the antiques the previous owner had stored there. We were accused of stealing it and had to spend the night in jail. There was a trial later, but we were acquitted. Of course, the parents of my students at Springside School didn't want me teaching there anymore. I was ready to quit that job anyway."

That spring Gillmer took her first trip west with Monty because she "wanted to see the desert." The women began their tour headed southwest, probably through Ohio and Missouri to Oklahoma before reaching New Mexico and Arizona. Years later I saw for myself the magical quality of the red land of New Mexico they drove into, the snaking, resolute force of the Rio Grande they crossed. As they looked down into the Grand Canyon, its majestic depths must have confirmed Gillmer's faith in a scale of reality and antiquity beyond the confines of her upbringing. I like to imagine her making the escape she had long desired—however temporary. I like to picture the western landscape coming alive for her, to visualize her hiking about the desert land and delighting in the spaciousness.

I can imagine the intensified "looking" she did in the West, studying the desert's complex curriculum, building the knowledge base she would need someday to document it thoroughly. For her, looking involved more than seeking a place to paint; it also meant taking a rigorous wilderness course in the field. Mary Austin called the desert the "Country of Lost Borders."[15] And it was these exciting, limitless sight lines—a relief from Philadelphia's finite perspective—that challenged Gillmer's artistic expression.

Although they enthralled her, these boundless spaces frustrated her classically trained abilities. She had a hard time containing the space on the small canvases she favored, accustomed as she was to replicating detail such as in a woodcut she had made a few years earlier, *Old Philadelphia Street,* with its complex accretion of buildings storied in times long past.

But with what eventually became an inevitable sense of connection and responsibility to the desert, she persisted until her perspective was equal to the challenges of this, her chosen subject. She became a dedicated student of the West's powerful landscape, which continually fascinated and occupied her as she repeated the course work with each trip she made that decade.

Still, she dutifully returned to Philadelphia from that trip in order to work and earn enough money to support subsequent treks, newly invigorated with images of the West's amazing possibilities.

During the Depression years, many "sisters of the road," surviving on their nerve and wits, joined hobos to ride in empty boxcars of trains speeding throughout the country.[16] Wanting to know that thrill, Gillmer once hopped a train in Baltimore and rode those rails a while. She sometimes went off alone on "safaris," camping and hiking in the Canadian mountains, getting away from "stuffy and self-satisfied" Germantown.

Both she and Monty loved antiques, so they peddled them around the Pennsylvania countryside from the back of an old jalopy Gillmer bought for fifty dollars. The antiques were easy to get because "lots of people were throwing out the old and buying golden oak furniture," Ella explained.

The women also carved small three-dimensional animal shapes from fine wood and painted them with careful detail. They sold these to Saks Fifth Avenue in New York City. Gillmer built a dollhouse for her niece who lived in Reno and painted sailing ships, anchors, and sailor's rope on fabric and sewed it into a bedspread for her nephew Bert. But of all the jobs she held during the Depression, most vivid in her mind was the design business she and Monty ran.

"Monty knew how to use tools. She used to follow her father around, and he taught her," Ella told me. So Gillmer and Monty remodeled and decorated basements for those "who had money to spend during the Depression," converting concrete-floor cellars into recreation rooms. Because they couldn't get any men to help with the carpentry, they learned to do it all themselves. They designed the interiors as well—a different theme for each family. "We made one Flash Gordon room and decorated the front of the bar like the inside of a spaceship, with instruments on it and everything. We painted big windows on the walls with the view showing what space looked like. Of course, we didn't know, but we could imagine. That was fun to do."

Her favorite project was a Mexican adobe house with a fake fireplace and adobe bricks made of papier-mâché. "I painted a Mexican with a big sombrero on the wall to welcome guests and in the small bathroom a face peering into the window. The people asked me to do it!" she added in her own defense.

When Ella next went west, she drove her old jalopy, again accompanied by Monty as well as two other single women from art school—Arrah Lee Gaul, one of her instructors, and Kate Maher, the school secretary. Enabled by the automobile, their freedom to move throughout the country must have given them a sense of legitimacy as women. They camped and painted along the way, setting up their tent and canvas chairs outside small towns, rendering the West's warmer light in air scented with the spiciness of crushed sage.

They must have sat around their camp in the evenings, talking about their emerging futures. I wondered what they said, how they felt about their own pluck, that courage it took to tramp around the country with the freedom of men. I wanted to know how it felt to paint that unsettled land *en plein air,* that mythic and capacious immensity that Canadian artist Emily Carr called "shouting but silent space."[17]

During the years I knew Ella, I longed to learn more about her life and intentions as a single woman. When I asked her what she thought about dating and the possibilities of marriage during her twenties and thirties, she told me that she "hadn't really dated" and had long planned on never marrying. I appreciated her privacy too much to push the issue, though I was curious about what motivated her resistance. Likewise, she asked nothing of my private life, of my decisions to leave a marriage, of my reasons for living alone.

Yet, when we talked of her past, I could easily recognize the disconnect between the twenty years she spent as a single adult and the following forty years she spent as a married one before she resumed her art, once again alone. It was during those single years she was most alive—most vibrant and full of her future. I imagine this energy existed, in tandem with the obvious—her youth—because she was solely responsible for herself, because she was not challenged by a partnership with a man, and, more critically, because she spent her work and play hours with others so like her.

Even under those circumstances, the prevailing pressures to marry in the 1920s and 1930s must have been overwhelming; to have defied them for so long clearly required the resistance to marriage that Gillmer claimed. Women who develop primary relationships with other women after adolescence often create deep bonds as they share the emotional and intellectual intimacies of their inner lives and as they give and receive empathetic support. Single women, especially, can come to rely on these associations for most of the meaning in their lives.

In those days Gillmer was thought of as odd by many of her family members. She was clearly unconventional. It was tempting to think that she would have preferred the company of women for a lifetime, for all her needs. Yet I never had the courage to ask for a forthright definition of her relationship with these women, especially with her best friend and business partner, Monty, whom Ella remained close to for years after she married Bill. Gender feelings are complicated; I wasn't sure Ella, in her late eighties, could access the emotional vicissitudes of her thirties, and I didn't want to offend her by asking more direct questions.

As Gillmer, Arrah Lee, Kate, and Monty sat around their campfire in the open western land those evenings in the mid-1930s, they were breaking taboos and rejecting a compulsory way of life, all habits characteristic in a culture of women.

The women saw Nevada for the first time on that trip and took photographs of the open space; on the back of one, Gillmer labeled it simply "a vast beauty." On the reverse of another, a small sepia-toned snapshot that anticipated the images of the desert she would paint forty years later—an expanse of sage-covered ground leading to a lake in front of distant mountains—she wrote, "Heat! This is a picture of heat. Not steaming heat, but parching baking heat. Dry Lake in the heat of summer on the desert. Just a snow-white sheet of alkali."

The women visited California's coast, another first for Gillmer on that trip, and watched the Pacific crash and foam against the steep cliffs of Big Sur, a coastline Ella later told me she appreciated for its lack of human defilement. On a stop at Donner Lake, near Tahoe, Gillmer took a photo of the regal mountains of the Sierra Nevada—the last hurrah of California's verdant majesty on the verge of Nevada's desert. On the back of the black-and-white snapshot she described the view lyrically: "6 a.m. of a beautiful misty morning in the high Sierra. Donner Lake, California, like a jewel blanketed with cloud, reposing peacefully in its setting of jagged mountains peaks. Spring, and the mountains, shedding their winter coats of white, veiled with mist thru which peeps visions of green."

The women then returned eastward reluctantly—the vastness of the West growing even larger and more compelling in memory as they drove back toward the East's narrow and prescribed propriety.

In Philadelphia Gillmer worked for the noted artist Paula Himmelsbach Balano, her former instructor at the Philadelphia School of Design for Women. Balano designed and produced stained glass for churches throughout the Philadelphia area, including the Chapel at Valley Forge. Gillmer worked in Balano's studio, painting figures, patterns, borders, and drapery on colored glass for fifty cents an hour.

"Balano was quite a woman, very independent, a marvelous artist. But she was a poor businesswoman. She would bid too low so she'd get the job, then she would put out her best work but get no money. The head of her shop scolded her sometimes and tried to get her to charge a better price."

Ella told me how much she admired Paula Balano, a woman twenty-seven years her senior whose work habits and independence impressed the young Gillmer. As a student at the Pennsylvania Academy of the Fine Arts, Balano had traveled to Greece to paint. "That's where she met and married her husband, a Greek who was supposed to be a lawyer, but he didn't like to work," Ella remembered. "She had to get up right after her child was born and go back to work." Paula Balano and Gillmer remained friends for the next twenty-five years.

Gillmer and Monty also worked together into the late 1930s in a business Monty started. A news article in the *Philadelphia Evening Public Ledger* tells of Monty's five-year-old enterprise creating "antiques." A photo accompanying the article shows Gillmer standing in Watson's workroom before a table saw. Monty described the work: "Basically, our job is to take a good reproduction and wreck it. We have to batter the daylights out of it, put years of wear and tear on it in a few minutes. But the battering must be scientific. Just any cuts and scars won't do. Certain defects are typical of old furniture." Somehow, during the same period, the women also found the time and energy to remodel apartment buildings in downtown Philadelphia, as always reinforcing the work ethic of their male-identified lifestyle.

"I came out west again in the late thirties, the year Alf Landon was running for president, and I remember it so well. I loved the West."

It was 1936, and Gillmer was headed once again westward, this time traveling with her mother, their 1930 Dodge pulling a camping trailer Gillmer had built.

Adelaide was fifty-nine years old and had finally decided she needed to learn to drive, her own desire for autonomy having overcome fears instilled by her late husband's car accident seventeen years earlier. The women took advantage of the wide western desert where Gillmer could safely instruct her mother. The West's open roads probably encouraged, as well, the speed and aggressiveness that would characterize Ella's driving when she lived in Spring City.

Adelaide and Gillmer were touring Zion National Park in southern Utah—most likely in awe of the desert varnish of rich carmine staining the high cliffs Ella would later paint—when they decided to go to Salt Lake City before driving on to Reno to see Adelaide's sister.

Salt Lake City drew Adelaide and Gillmer for a specific reason. Shortly before Ella's father, George Albert Smyth, died in 1919, an apostle of the Mormon Church, Richard Roswell Lyman, a distant cousin of Ella's father, had written her father requesting genealogical information about the Smyth family. So, with that connection in their minds, the women drove north from Zion on Interstate 15, passing the small outlying farming communities of Parowan, Scipio, and Juab, towns named by the original Mormon pioneer settlers.

Ella liked to tell the story of visiting the church headquarters in Salt Lake City during that trip west with her mother. "Richard Lyman escorted us upstairs to meet the Mormon apostle George Albert Smith, who was standing at a lectern addressing the Relief Society. The man introduced mother to this roomful of women as Mrs. George Albert Smyth. That got a laugh from everyone." His implication that Adelaide was a second wife was humorous because the church had officially renounced the doctrine of polygamy in 1890 as a tradeoff for securing statehood, though, then as now, the practice continued among fundamentalist Mormons.

The women stayed in Salt Lake City long enough to learn about the Mormon lifestyle, a culture that, like the Smyths', emphasized family, education, and industry. Other parallels between Salt Lake City and her birthplace and hometown in Pennsylvania must have resonated for Gillmer.

William Penn, who founded Germantown in 1681, and Brigham Young, who established Salt Lake City in 1847, were both God-fearing visionaries committed to providing their faithful followers with sanctuaries from religious persecution. Both men—multitalented and with radical utopian ideals and determined spirits—designed their respective cities with streets laid out in grids in precise, symmetrical right angles. Whereas the land on which Germantown was founded lay between a bay and a freshwater lake, rich with river valleys, rolling mountain slopes, and dense forests, the Salt Lake Valley was characterized by inhospitable, arid deserts and formidable mountains.

Perhaps Gillmer realized these parallels and contrasts that summer in Salt Lake City and admired the merit underlying Brigham Young's endeavors. At any rate, she kept favorable impressions of Utah and its dominant religion and culture prominent in her mind, along with the more stirring images of the desert's immense beauty, as she drove her mother across the salt flats to Reno. Then, leaving a landscape Gillmer would not visit again for nearly thirty years, she headed east once again, her promise to return firmly lodged in her heart.

At the end of the Depression, the culture of women that had shaped Gillmer's life for more than two decades ended. When Gillmer and Monty needed a carpenter to help them with apartments they were remodeling, an Englishman, William Francis Bailey Peacock, answered their advertisement. He added a new name and a conventional structure to Gillmer's life, one that would keep her grounded in the East for another thirty years.

Lehi Roller Mills. OIL, 24″ X 20″. COURTESY OF JOE AND LEE BENNION.

LEHI ROLLER MILLS

*Everything here is expectation, the premonition that even
the ordinary is likely to be invested with such shining
individuality that it takes on the character of the remarkable, the
rare, the awesome. Unless the potential for surprise
has been leached from you, you cannot be lonely here,
merely solitary in your humanness.*
—THOMAS WATKINS, *Stonetime*

BY MIDSUMMER the Great Basin desert is already parched, its vegetation tinder dry. People sometimes scan the horizon anxiously, watching for smoke. The idea of a wheat field, the plenty symbolized by a harvest, seemed incongruous on the hot July day when I pulled off I-15 at Lehi, twenty-five miles south of Salt Lake, and parked in front of the Lehi Roller Mills, a complex wooden structure set alongside railroad tracks close to the freeway. Completed in 1905, the year Ella was born, and still producing flour from local wheat, the mill is a solid presence in the small town of Lehi. But until I saw it through Ella's paintings, in all the times I'd driven past it I'd never really noticed it. Now I sat in my car and thought about the fading red sign identifying it in block letters as the LEHI ROLLER MILLS, straddling both sides of one corner of the building, and considered its two green silos, each advertising a brand of flour—Turkey Red Flour and Peacock Flour.

During the years she lived in Utah, Ella made at least five paintings of the Lehi Roller Mills, all large for her—fifteen by twenty-five inches—and richly hued. In every one I saw, she painted the right-most silo advertising Peacock Flour so close to the right margin of the painting that the word *Peacock* was incomplete—her nod at modesty, I thought. But in one painting—the one meant for her son—she reversed the position of the silos and painted the Peacock silo with the name complete.

The painting I know best belongs to Joe and Lee Bennion, Ella's first, a 1930s stylistic treatment of the venerable structure painted in the late 1970s. The sky is full of creamy clouds, the wood siding of the mill pale maize. The composition is perfect, the viewer's eye being pulled into the painting on the left, attracted to the height and deep brown of a telephone pole and the dark-red sign. The painting's focus seems to be the sign on the main structure; only secondarily does the viewer notice the text on the deep-green silos.

Besides the obvious connection to her name, something else impelled Ella to drive from Spring City seventy-five miles north to Lehi so many times and park partially hidden under the freeway overpass day after day in order to make meaning of the considerable structure. She was probably drawn to it, as she was to other period buildings, because of its age and function. She loved old things, admired hard work, and respected productivity.

Ella was a student of art when it was a compliment for a woman to be said to paint in a "masculine style," one that focused on bold subjects and employed large, expansive brush strokes. Her work was never delicate or "precious" in any way. But her style was not a matter of adaptation to the prevailing artistic taste of the times; she preferred it. Neither was she rankled by other attitudes and practices we might now consider sexist. Ella taught drafting for a correspondence school during the 1950s and readily complied with instructions to sign her responses to student work with her first initial and last name only, so the students wouldn't know their instructor was a woman. But she had already adopted the practice early in her career: my print of *The New Jersey Shore* is signed in pencil, androgynously, "E. G. Smyth 1927."

After Ella moved to Utah, she did not succumb to romantic renderings of the rough landscape. She ignored spectacular subjects that attracted other painters—the dramatic glacier-cut Horseshoe Mountain in Sanpete, the nineteenth-century dome of the state capitol, or Salt Lake's castlelike temple. She saw, instead, handsome reality in scrubby land, and substance in its weedy native plants. Her work gave tactile strength to heavy farm equipment and enduring old buildings such as the one before me.

That afternoon as I sat in my car contemplating one of Ella's favorite subjects, I thought about her attraction to the opportunities and competency of men, to their ability to command their own labor and control their own yield. Likewise, her assertive approach to and interpretation of the world seemed to come naturally to her, perhaps elicited from a deep-seated claim to gender equality. Hers was not a political or fashionable stance, but simply a practical one. And Ella, a woman who never suffered nonsense in any form, fully expected to engage the world as a person and an artist, unhampered by her sex.

Likewise, she eschewed pretense, seeing it as dishonest and frivolous. Ella's Salt Lake friend Rachel Kirk had told me the previous day about a visit she and Ella made during the 1960s to the headquarters of the Relief Society, the women's organization of the Mormon Church, in Salt Lake City. The foyer featured formal portraits of the women leaders of the organization.

Ella, bewildered and likely bemused, confronted a receptionist, "Can you tell me why all the women in these paintings are smiling?" Her challenge to what she saw as an affectation was typical and sprang easily from her abiding discomfort with pretension. Ella's lively smile burst out readily—at something funny I said, at her own jokes, at her own foibles. But it wasn't something she flashed for effect.

Most of what she did was for a purpose—because it worked for her. Comfortable with the lesson in that thought, I started my car and headed south once again.

As I drove through Thistle Canyon, the noise and congestion in Utah County behind me, and entered again Sanpete County's hushed desert, I recalled Ella's painting *Surveying in Thistle* showing Highway 89's reconstruction, an immense project that took years to complete after the town of Thistle and the highway through it were destroyed in the flood of 1983. Her image shows working men, nearly dwarfed by the red cliffs, surveying for a new road to be built high above the flooded canyon.

It seemed, suddenly, that Ella's favorite subjects were arrayed all around me: men and machines, cranes and trucks, barns and vestiges of barns. I passed fields filled with five-foot-high rolled hay and alfalfa, scrub oak–dappled yellow land spreading for miles before rugged mountains, and an old two-story stone house hollow of life— all part of Ella's vision of hard work and efficient yield.

After Mt. Pleasant, I slowed down for the last few miles into Spring City. The poplar trees were in full leaf. The sky was a deep blue and streaked with clouds like freshly laundered white shirtsleeves billowing on a clothesline.

My summer visits had developed into a pleasant routine. Ella and I had tacitly established a pattern for our time working together. I knew she liked to work alone in the mornings—painting if the sky was interesting, looking at the landscape if not, or completing a painting in her studio. She enjoyed watching television privately after lunch, and I knew she liked company in the afternoons—all of which was ideal for me as well.

I pulled into Craig and M'Lisa Paulsen's driveway. This time they had space for me in a two-story cottage on their property, a former coal house Craig had restored. It was charming, made of large blocks of limestone with arched stone lintels. A small roofed canopy carved with a heart protected a nineteenth-century wine-red door that was embellished with a bas-relief bow-tied wreath. It was small inside—a kitchen and a bathroom downstairs with the bedroom above. I set up my writing on an old wooden table in the kitchen facing a window that looked out onto a small flower garden, its bright-red torch lilies peeking above the sill.

I thought it might take me a few nights to get used to the farm sounds, and it did. The first night one of the curly-horned sheep in the adjacent corral emitted a series of long, moaning coughs, persistent and loud enough to keep me awake for hours.

The next morning I worked peacefully, looking forward to the date I'd made with Ella on the phone the night before. She had surprised me by inviting me to meet her where she was painting and gave me specific directions where to find her working in one of her favorite spots along Pigeon Hollow Road. "I'll be there at 2:00 P.M. exactly," she pointedly told me.

So that afternoon I drove south out of Spring City and turned left onto a dirt side road at a particularly gnarly sagebrush skeleton as directed and looked for Ella's car. I thought she might be near the old house she said she would be painting, but I couldn't see her anywhere.

I sat in my car a minute, waiting as the dust swirls settled, and regarded the only structure in miles of open desert, a leaning, broken-down stone and brick shedlike building with a roof nearly destroyed. Was that the house in Pigeon Hollow she'd painted so often? Was that what drew her so diligently to this forlorn spot?

Finally I saw her gray Chevy Nova, nearly indistinguishable from the subtly toned landscape, parked in the middle of a large fenced and overgrown field that had to have been someone's property. She seemed so far from the old house, yet when I at last reached her, I saw that the bleak brick structure was indeed what she was painting.

Sitting in her car with her canvas propped up on the seat beside her and wearing her trademark brown fedora, she was peering through her windshield at the house— her hand poised and ready to convey her respect. She quickly put down her brush when I reached her car, and said she was ready for a break. I saw she had already begun to sketch with her paintbrush directly onto the primed canvas.

"Isn't this nice?" she asked, indicating her subject. "See, the sky changes every time you look at it. Isn't that a beautiful old building?"

I looked at the empty structure, its bricks missing randomly throughout, nearly collapsed in this desolate place, its haunting loneliness exuding through the granite windowsills.

"Hmmm," I ventured.

"It has just gradually gone to pieces," she said. "And when the roof goes, then the whole building goes if they don't fix it. And that side of the roof is bare.... It's a mess." It didn't look to me as though anyone would be fixing it anytime soon.

Ella must have painted that old building dozens of times, in all seasons and from all angles and perspectives. I wondered what attracted her to it.

She told me, "Oh, it's the whole weather situation—the heavy sky or the fog you're looking through. Once I stopped to paint that when it was very misty and snowy. You could just see through this fog to the mountains, the house, and the foreground. And I got out my paints in a hurry and before I was through, it was buried in snow. I got something out of it, though."

I wondered, however, if it was less the atmosphere than the ruin before her that spoke to her so poignantly and so often over the years as she herself aged and succumbed to gravity. We agreed she should get back to work, and I left, telling her I would come over the next afternoon. Tramping through the sandy ground back to my car, I had the sense I'd been privy to an intimacy, that I'd witnessed a woman completely content with herself, with her element.

"Right now I know I'm by myself too much. I have been told that. And I never was a social person anyway, but in the late afternoons and evenings I get—well, I just feel awful. I get kind of lonely here. I miss Bill." She sounded apologetic.

We were settled in her living room again, Ella sitting in the corner of her sofa beside a small table holding her heavy black dial telephone and a pile of acrostic games she regularly ordered from the Penny Press. I sat across the room from her on a bamboo side chair.

"Tell me about meeting Bill," I suggested now.

"Golly, I met my husband over a hammer and a saw! Monty and I hired him to help us on the apartments we were remodeling. And it was interest at first sight."

Since I'd never known Bill and she talked so little of her life with him, he had become, I suppose, fairly incidental in my mind. In my mythology of Ella Peacock, I suddenly realized, she had always been alone in her purposeful existence. But the reality was that Bill had shared forty years of her life.

She went to the antique desk and returned with a manila envelope. Inside was a copy of Bill's life story that Ella had long ago written out in longhand as Bill dictated.

William F. B. Peacock, who had lied about his age and enlisted in World War I in England as a fifteen year old, immigrated to the United States as a young man. He worked at odd jobs as a carpenter and was forty when he took a fancy to Gillmer Smyth.

"He admired women who could do things," Ella remembered. "I was thirty-four and wasn't worried about getting married. In fact, I never planned to. And Bill didn't plan to get tied up with anybody, either. He was a little bit jittery, and I think he was scared. But he was a real person, and I fell for him. There wasn't any question in my mind. He kind of brought me to life."

Despite the disapproval of Ella's mother—"I guess she thought I should marry someone who knew how to act in society"—Bill and Gillmer married in a small ceremony in 1939.

Interestingly, their only wedding picture shows them standing back-to-back. It's an ordinary setting, outdoors in front of a split-rail fence. Bill is wearing a dark suit, Ella a dark skirt and long-sleeved white collared shirt. Their hands are clasped, their gaze downward—a notable divergence from a typical wedding photo. The image, perhaps, presages the atypical union and relationship to come.

I would imagine it was complicated for Gillmer to change her direction so fundamentally. Perhaps by resorting to the convention of marriage, she hoped to ensure a safer passage into her future. I wonder whether Monty felt betrayed by Gillmer's decision, as women often do when long and comfortable friendships alter significantly when a man comes into the picture. Monty herself never married but lived on a ranch on Lake Wallenpaupack in the Pocono Mountains where Bill and Ella frequently visited her.

After living two years in the family's Harvey Street house, which the newlyweds had bought from Gillmer's mother, having helped convert it into apartments, Bill and Gillmer moved to North Wales in Bucks County just north of Philadelphia. The countryside promised escape from the city's polluted air and hence relief for Bill's health problems caused by exposure to mustard gas during the Great War. There they built a brick home where they raised rabbits and chickens to sell.

When the United States entered World War II and the government created new opportunities for women, Gillmer took advantage of an offer of free course work in drafting. She worked at engineering firms near Philadelphia until their only child, Bailey, was born in 1944. When Bailey was six, Gillmer returned to drafting, working in New York designing wiring diagrams that the firm sold to *Voice of America*.

The Peacocks bought a dairy farm in 1952 in Wayne County in northern Pennsylvania, even though, Ella claimed, "neither of us knew how to milk cows." After some initial failures, they learned what kind of cows to buy and how to handle them. Bill was particularly happy on the farm where he named every cow and sometimes found time to hunt, always accompanied by his dogs. Bill taught Ella to make pies and bread, and together they raised enough crops that they seldom needed to buy groceries. They kept many cats and, fittingly, peacocks—birds whose showy, strutting behavior, however, contrasted directly to Bill and Gillmer's modest sensibilities.

The long hours of physical labor, the punishing isolation of winter, and financial hardship combined to threaten their dream of idyllic rural life. After three years working alongside Bill on the farm, Ella returned to drafting at a variety of firms in New Jersey, Scranton, and nearby Honesdale, Pennsylvania. Finally, needing "to save the farm," she took a drafting job in New York City, living nearby with her sister during the week and returning to the farm by train on Friday nights. I can imagine Ella's resolute dutifulness on those train rides—how it must have obscured her longing for the leisure to pursue her art.

I found some letters Bill wrote to Ella during her absences from home. He often encouraged her in his correspondence and lamented the fact that she wasn't able to spend time painting. And he called her by a variety of endearments—his most enduring, "Rollo," remained inexplicable in its source. "Well, Toots," he wrote in one, "keep your chin up and don't worry about us here. Look after yourself for you know I do worry about you and cannot think of anyone but you." His frequent and pointed support suggested to me that he might have felt responsible for her predicament, and, most clearly, compassionate for her in her loneliness.

In all, Ella worked at drafting for a quarter of a century before retiring and moving west. "I regretted not quitting drafting sooner. I could have," Ella told me. "It was always in the back of my mind to move out west. I was just waiting to get back to painting."

Waiting for what? I wondered. For the burden of the farm mortgage to be lifted? For her son, Bailey, to leave home? There were probably a hundred other good reasons besides. Why did it seem that women of every age found themselves waiting for their lives to begin, waiting to get back to some version of themselves they used to know? Were gender imperatives so potent that our real selves went dormant for whole decades? At age fifty, I was three years into the project of uncovering myself from the weight of my own choices and asking myself these same questions.

◈◈◈

Ella and I talked on another hot afternoon in her cool living room, the foot-thick adobe walls once again providing insulation. I was curious about her initial encounter with the place she had decided to make her own.

"Bill and I read an article about Spring City in the *Deseret News* when we lived in Salt Lake, and took a drive down here one weekend," she began. "We walked down the streets of Spring City and saw the whole town, but we didn't see any people around." Bill and Ella stopped to talk to a man working on his house, just three blocks south of the town's center. He told them most people in town were at a church picnic. "We asked him if there were any places for sale around here, and he said he didn't know of any place—most everybody was keeping their old houses. Pretty soon, he showed us around his house. I liked the house as soon as I saw it, and so did Bill. We liked old places.

"'If you are interested in this, I'll sell it to you for thirty-five,' he said. I thought thirty-five thousand dollars was a little much for this place, for this area and the condition the house was in. But he meant thirty-five hundred dollars. I could hardly believe it. The next Saturday we came down and bought it. And we were told later thirty-five hundred dollars was too much to pay, but I'm glad we did."

So Ella and Bill became Utahns after all. And for the first time in her adult life she called herself Ella to strangers, ironically reclaiming a hint of femininity, perhaps in acquiescence to small-town tradition. The Peacocks lived in their Airstream trailer while they remodeled the old adobe house. Bill installed the ductwork for the oil furnace they added, and Ella helped him install the roof. He built the brick fireplace and the bookcase beside it. "We had to make it livable, you see."

Ella told me about the original wallpaper in the living and dining room: "It was pretty remarkable—dark, flowery, and all dirty. The walls needed painting, but we would have to scrape off all the wallpaper first. We didn't have the time for that, so I washed the walls and painted them with a dove-gray paint I mixed."

Ella told it so casually—the story of painting the gray walls and the captivating border—the most distinctive feature of her home's interior and, in a way, her first interpretative landscape in Sanpete County.

Using earth tones naturally found in desert plants and soil—soft turquoise, maize, clay red, and sage green—the narrow, waist-high border frieze around the circumference of the living and dining rooms detailed a repeated pattern of Native American images, depicting such icons as an Indian on horseback, a rising sun, and an ancient fish. It is this border that I was to find so emblematic of Ella's distinctive spirit—her sense for subtle color, a love of natural shapes, and a naturalist's aesthetic for pattern and imagery.

Bill and Ella filled the old adobe with their antiques, family heirlooms such as the early-nineteenth-century Governor Winthrop desk and the Sheraton drop-leaf side table as well as other old things Ella had collected during the Depression. Two of her treasures were artist's proofs of etchings by Frederic Remington that had belonged to Ella's father, one dated 1905, the year Ella was born. Unusual in Spring City, the Peacocks' fine old furniture conveyed a sense of Ella's East Coast aristocratic heritage, but the pieces seemed relieved of their respectable burden in this humble setting.

The effect of the Peacocks' elegant furnishings in their modest house brought to my mind the celebrated advice from William Morris, the pioneering leader of the British Arts and Crafts movement: to "have nothing in your house that you do not know to be useful or believe to be beautiful." Likewise, Ella's personal style was suited to the plain and relatively meager setting of Spring City. While she didn't determine her own worth, or anyone else's, on superficialities, she added an uncommon element to the town's simple character. Her sensibility, so typical of the Arts and Crafts movement, infused everything about her with a subdued stylishness.

The next afternoon was still very hot, the air especially dry. I realized I had started to get used to aridity, to finally appreciate the clarity of thought the parched air seemed to give me. I was content now in Sanpete Valley, although I knew it was the place, not the community, I identified with. I still knew few people who lived here.

Other than the Bennions, who had become good, trusted friends, I was acquainted with two other people in Spring City. Ron Staker, the director of the Fairview Museum, welcomed my calls and visits, freely offering information and advice in response to my random requests. Likewise, I knew Ella's neighbor, water-colorist Osral Allred, but only enough to share my concerns about Ella's welfare.

Other people I encountered—the librarians, the farmers on the road, the editor of the local paper—all seemed to merely abide my presence, to respond to my questions with dispatch, to notice I didn't belong. The day the Bennions' elder daughter got married, I parked my car right in front of the church. After the wedding when everyone spilled out the front door and mingled, I overheard one man say, "Let's see if we can guess who has the California license plates." By that time I had no illusions that I could "pass" as a local, nor did I want to, particularly.

I could understand the dichotomy Ella must have felt as she effortlessly revealed her westerner's character yet struggled so to remain true to her sense of self in this small town. Even though she seemed to have come home when she came to Sanpete County and seemed such a natural there, she still struggled with a middle child's sense of displacement. She had never completely fitted in, had never been entirely accepted by most of the community.

Her few really close friends—the Bennions, her good friend Helen Madsen, her neighbors the Allreds, and Paul and Ann Larsen—all loved her because they loved her passion and strength and understood the value in her vision. Helen Madsen talked as though Ella were her heroine, telling me earnestly about a trip the two women took to Grafton to paint. They checked into a motel in nearby Springdale and found their room unsatisfactory—unclean and shabby. Helen told me that Ella marched right back to the office and told the manager they "weren't two old ladies he could mistreat." It worked, and Ella and Helen were given a better room.

Yet, when I asked Ella about her fit into the community, she responded wryly. "See, I'm a newcomer here. I've been here twenty years, and I'm still a newcomer. A columnist in the *Pyramid* wrote about this. I said to her, 'You know it's a crime to be a newcomer, don't you?'"

We both laughed, and Ella continued telling me about her sense of not meeting the community's expectations for an old lady. Since she had dreaded social events all her life, invitations to "club" or programs for senior citizens unnerved her. "I don't like programs, do you?" she asked. I just laughed but knew exactly what she meant. "There's a senior citizen's dinner tonight, and I don't know what to do," Ella worried aloud.

Then, without waiting for advice, she changed the subject. "Do you know what happened once? My home teachers [emissaries of the local Mormon congregation] sat right in this room and asked me if there wasn't something they could do for me. Then they offered to pull out the sagebrush plants Bill and I dug up in the desert and planted here." Home teachers are prompted by the church to help those they visit, but Ella was hardly the sort of needy widow they were accustomed to.

Though the many artists who lived in and visited Spring City valued her dedication to her work, most in the community didn't understand why she preferred to spend her time painting. Others were blatantly insensitive, like the one who cautioned her, "You should paint *after* you do church work!" Ella repeatedly consternated a succession of home teachers whom Joe Bennion said the ward's bishop kept replacing, none of them able to fulfill their mission of service to this uncommon elderly woman.

It was likewise difficult for the Allreds to get Ella to come next door to their home for dinner; she didn't like others to fuss over her and took pride in her self-reliance. Hers was a sincere independence—she didn't cave and she didn't compromise. But maintaining that stance was hard on her; clearly, she felt vulnerable at times.

"Look here," she said, poking at the brown age spots and bruises on her forearms. "I'm falling apart." Her feelings bruised easily as well. Slights and prying questions frustrated her. She explained some of her indignation in a letter to her son, telling him about a Sunday-school teacher who told her she should learn to read lips when she told him she couldn't hear his soft voice. In a community that so highly valued family relationships—multigenerational Sunday dinners, family reunions, and birthday celebrations—she was an oddity, a widow without discernable family ties. When she was honored for her work or in the hospital recovering from one of her car accidents, people asked where her son was, why he wasn't in attendance. Such questions were especially wounding; Ella was already sensitive to Bailey's indifference to her work. With only one child and no grandchildren, she had no photos to pass around with pride and no one to "serve," which, as Ella reported, one grandmother in town said was *her* sole purpose in life.

Ella was an anomaly among her contemporaries in other ways: she told me more than once about a woman in town who disapproved of wives making more money than their husbands, telling Ella that she quit her job as soon as her salary exceeded her husband's. "Why, I always made more than Bill, and it never bothered either of us!" Ella said.

Some in town didn't appreciate Ella's devotion to her dog, Jeff. In Sanpete County people generally keep their dogs outside, but Jeff was important to Ella, the object of many chats and much faithful companionship during her long years living alone. She once wrote to her son about encountering a pony on the highway when she was out walking. "He walked the whole way home with us, Jeff on my one side and the pony on the other." Imagining the scene brought me pleasure—Ella and Jeff and the pony, lone figures having discovered in one another a gentle, abiding presence beyond the expectations and censure of others.

That quiet day in Spring City I felt a spiritual twinning with Ella as I remembered my discomfort and the claustrophobic feelings I'd had years earlier visiting my husband's family in Fairview. Now, after these years spent with Ella, I could understand the solace and compensation she found by herself in the capaciousness of this place and its rhythms—its big sky filling suddenly with storm clouds, the steady hum of tractors and gossip.

The next day, as agreed, Ella and I went out "looking" together. She climbed into my car rather gingerly, clearly unused to the passenger seat, and refused to buckle the seat belt when I suggested it.

"I don't like being tied in," she announced resolutely as I backed out of her driveway, crushing a swath in the fallen pinecones. "Listen, we were building our house in Bucks County, and we bought this old truck to move stuff. My son was a baby, and I needed to go to the station to meet Bill. I started the truck and it burst into flames in the motor, and I had to get Bailey untangled and it took too long. If he had been loose, it would have been much faster. I didn't know how soon the truck was going to blow up! So, I don't like being tied in."

We passed the remains of an old house just a few blocks from hers, blackened boards barely erect, light showing through each one. Its condition reminded her of a house she liked on Wales Road, between the nearby towns of Wales and Fountain Green. "It's a beautiful old place. It's not redbrick but a lighter brick. The way it's built is perfect, and it was in good shape. I painted it twice. I just went back that way to see it yesterday when I went out to look, and here it was just a pile of rubble. They had demolished it. That had a good roof on it and everything. It was sickening. It could have been restored and made into a house because it hadn't started to fall down yet."

By then we were driving south on Highway 89, approaching the next town, Ephraim. A two-block-long stand of sixty Russian black willows lined the roadway near the town cemetery, "I love those trees. I hope they don't trim them." Standing as sentinels to the town's entrance, the hundred-year-old trees, I subsequently learned, were originally planted from seedlings brought across the plains by early pioneers. It would be only a few years later, after Ella left Utah, that local activists would have to fight to keep the trees from being leveled. And I'm thankful Ella never lived to see the sprawling new Wal-Mart that was eventually built next to Ephraim's historic old cemetery, its floodlights glaring across acres of empty parking lot throughout the night.

We came back into Spring City from its north end, passing a very large new house. I thought it was well designed and built, but its elevation was disproportionate and its character discordant in this small farming town. It was painted deep maize to resemble a Tuscan villa, with huge carved cathedral doors imported from Italy. I mentioned that the owners had one of her paintings in their kitchen. Ella said, "Someone in that house wouldn't like my paintings. Well, they *shouldn't* like them!" This was but one of several houses recently built in Spring City; others featured broad beveled-glass windows and slick varnished front doors.

"They're monstrosities," Ella said, her intense blue eyes fairly glaring, "just built for show by new people from California. I think they were kicked out of California. Those houses certainly don't belong here. We need more zoning laws, or this town will be kicked out of the National Historical District."

"In Philadelphia," she continued, "if we wanted to change our front porch, we had to draw up plans and submit them for approval. I had two men come to my door the other day who wanted to side my house with aluminum. Can you imagine? I told them I bought this house because it's an adobe house and I want it to stay an adobe house."

We sat in the old theater chairs on her front porch for a while after we returned, not talking much, just listening to the breeze stir her large maple tree and watching the horse graze in the field across the street. Ella stroked Pussy Cat, her long gnarled fingers passing slowly through the soft black fur.

As I opened the front door, I asked Ella about the brass knocker mounted on it. "We brought that with us from Philadelphia," she told me. Now dark with tarnish, its simple design seemed an integral fixture on the century-old pine door that had been hand-grained, most likely the work of C. C. A. Christensen, the noted Utah pioneer artist. I pulled the old door closed behind us then and stood just inside for a moment while my eyes adjusted to the familiar muted light.

When Ella and Bill moved to Salt Lake City in the late 1960s, it had been nearly forty years since Ella had devoted herself to her art. She enrolled in a figure-drawing class, beginning again, as artists do, with the human form. At a time when most schools across the country were using nude models for life classes, this Utah school had not quite refined the practice, as Ella explained to me.

"They had a nude model, but the instructor didn't know how to run it. You know, the model poses for a certain amount of time and then rests. It's professional for the model to put on a robe and walk around then. They don't walk around without any clothes on and talk to people. But she didn't know that, and the instructor didn't know that.

"Anyway, this one student I think was there just to converse with a nude model because he would go right up on the platform and have a conversation with her when she was resting, and that wasn't right; it wasn't professional at all. Here, I want to show you something."

It was an article about the San Francisco artist Trevor Southey. "I like his work," she said. "He's very fine. He's got something. Don't you think?"

Then she got to her point: "The first time I ever saw one of his paintings was at the Salt Lake airport, a mural with nudes, and they had to take it down. Someone in the newspaper said, 'Anybody looking at that would go out and commit a crime.' Isn't that ridiculous? I feel like saying, 'Where's your brain?'"

I read the article about Southey aloud. He was a well-respected artist, and, at the time of the airport mural controversy, an instructor at Brigham Young University (BYU). The article related BYU's insistence that Southey cover strategic body parts on his nude paintings, a demand that actually prompted inventive imagery in his work. Ella listened carefully, and when I finished she said, "BYU has one of my nude paintings. I talked to a man who ran an exhibition there once and asked him why they put bikinis on the models in the life-drawing classes. He said, 'We have to be careful with the older people.' BYU has to keep things acceptable, but they will gradually get out of that." I wasn't so sure. It seemed to me that the more our society gave up adherence to meaningless rules, the more conservatively reactionary the Mormon Church became.

Ella said, "Somebody here asked me why I wanted to paint a nude, why not a body with clothes on?" She looked at me with her wide, intelligent eyes and pointed to my arm. "Just think of the human skin, the flesh; when you're painting a piece of tweed, it's not nearly as interesting. The human body is beautiful. And I think when they put these darn little things—these bikinis—on them, it makes it more unacceptable than if they were nude. It's ridiculous."

Ella's most keenly felt and most pointed opinions concerned narrow attitudes toward art. It especially annoyed her that critics claimed to see sexual imagery in Georgia O'Keeffe's flower paintings. Ella's classical art training was too ingrained to allow her to suffer what she saw as foolishness about art.

I asked if she would show me how she carved and built her distinctive frames. "I can do that," she said. "I have some work I can do to show you."

So we went into her kitchen where I sat on an old wooden chair while she stood at the alcove and began to work on one of her hallmark frames. She told me about her process while she worked fitting the moldings together.

I remembered Joe Bennion saying she salvaged wood from the local dump when she first moved to Sanpete County and in later years she drove to Salt Lake to get fine-grained sugar pine that she cut into sticks for the molding.

"Now, since my saw broke, Dale Peel cuts the sticks from basswood just the size I want and miters them for me. Then he rabbets them," she told me contentedly.

Dale Peel, a local craftsman who makes traditional custom Mormon pine furniture, worked for eight years cutting sticks for Ella. Rabbetting the molding creates an open groove in the back of the sticks, a step in the wood that holds the painting in the frame. He used the more traditional basswood for Ella's molding, finer grained, but soft like sugar pine and easier to carve. Dale told me later that, for the previous five years, every time Ella came into his shop to pick up the sticks he'd prepared, she would say, acknowledging her advanced age, "This will probably be the last time I build frames."

After she glued the four sticks together, Ella put the painting into the frame to see what pattern of grooves would best present the painting and made pencil marks on the frame as a guide for her knife. Then, after removing the painting and working with her old tools, she carved a profile of long grooves into the frame to make a pattern of relief in the wood.

"What's in this?" I asked about a messy can holding a gelatinous-looking substance on her workbench. After the frame was glued together, carved, and sanded, Ella explained, it was coated it with a thin coat of warm rabbit-skin glue—actually made from the collagen of French rabbits.

"I heat the glue in the double boiler. It finishes the wood, so the wood doesn't change color when you tone it. That way the paint won't soak in or make the finish spotty. So, there are two rabbits in each frame!"

Next, she toned her frames with a "wash" from her "slime jar," the mayonnaise jar that collected the leftover paint she scraped from her palette each time she cleaned it.

After the frame was toned, she mixed colors to complement the image, selecting one or two of the grooves to emphasize the painting's characteristic tonal subtlety. This accent on the frame was applied while it held the canvas so she could get it just right; in so doing she crafted the complete harmony of form and function.

She talked lovingly of her carving tools, reminding me, "I've had these since I was in art school. Now I don't have as many. I found out which ones I needed and gave away the others." She asked me if I would take them to the knife sharpener in Salt Lake City when I left that week. "He'll return them by mail when he finishes with them," she assured me.

She was unusually relaxed as she talked about making her signature frames. Explaining the process was easier for her than answering my interview questions, probably because she didn't have to remember anything; frame making was a part of her physical memory, and she could effortlessly describe what her hands were doing and why.

Artists and collectors alike agreed that her frames were an integral part of her paintings, a sort of folk art that gently echoed the landscape's wildness in their rough-hewn quality. She knew this, but she must have also gleaned pleasure from the task because it was something she could do, like painting outdoors, with complete confidence in her purpose.

While she worked, I started looking at some slides of her paintings that I found on the kitchen table, projecting each one onto the kitchen wall. I commented that none had dates or titles. "Oh, yes. I should have written down more things. Can you help me with that?" So I marked some as well as recorded her memories of painting them or the comments she made about a particular place as they were illuminated on the wall.

Some of my favorite paintings are those she seemed to have painted herself into, like the *Lehi Roller Mills* that shows her resolute presence. "I found the best place to paint the Lehi Roller Mills; I stand under the freeway where no one can see me. Now they've built a fast-food restaurant in front of it. That spoils it."

On another slide was a painting of a large yellow rough-terrain crane, its ungainly main boom idle in soft afternoon light on fields it had just worked. Bold dark-blue and ocher mountains rose even larger behind it.

The Building of Callao depicts four workingmen full of life and activity—carrying heavy logs, building a roof, chopping with axes. Its large figures were unusual in Ella's paintings, the Van Gogh–like curving lines, detail, and rich colors in tapered brush strokes marking it as an early painting, "probably made in the 1970s—oh, I can't remember!"

I asked her about one sketchy scene, a hazy rendition of a brick house. "Oh, that one. That's a floperoo." She agreed with me about the high quality of a painting of the muted atmosphere of the Grafton Cemetery in southern Utah just outside Zion National Park. She had painted the cemetery's substance in her later style and calm palette. Sturdy old tombstones, some weathered and fallen, aged under a brooding sky that cast solemnity over the lonely scene.

"Grafton is a nice spot. I used to go there with Helen before she married her boyfriend. We would take my dog, Jeffery, with us and stay in a motel and paint. Now I don't have anyone to go with."

After Bill and Ella moved to Spring City, Ella was eager to pick up her brush again. "At first I was sneaking painting. I didn't want anybody to see me because I wanted to get back to doing it. I didn't want to advertise the fact. I was feeling my way, just interested in working. I wasn't thinking a bit about anything else, exhibiting or selling or anything else."

I recall Joe Bennion telling me that when he went to her house to invite her to show her paintings in a BYU exhibit of his pottery, he was amazed at the number of paintings she had hanging in the living room and studio. She had been painting for ten years virtually without showing anyone her work. Joe had to persuade Ella to go to the reception on opening night where she sold about seven canvases "to people who collected LeConte Stewart and Maynard Dixon," Joe recollected.

"I was flabbergasted at the first show," Ella told me, "when these people came up to meet me and here were these names like Gary Smith that I had read about and had never seen before. I was surprised really. I had a good start. It's good to get a boost."

Another invitation to show her work came unbidden. In 1984, Robert Redford invited her to exhibit in his first Utah Artists at Sundance series. She showed nine paintings. But when he asked her to contribute to a subsequent exhibit the following year—the only woman with twenty-four male artists—she declined, worried about her growing inability to converse intelligently in public.

Penny L. Perlmutter, the director of Maxwell Galleries in San Francisco, juried the art for the Springville Museum's April Salon in 1984. "Your work made a particularly strong impression on me," she wrote and offered Ella gallery representation.[18] Ella subsequently sent the gallery six of her paintings. But after a few months she asked for them back, telling Perlmutter only that she "needed them."

Although this opportunity could have readily broadened Ella's market, she was uncomfortable with the business of art and needed, somehow, to be personally connected with her buyers. Her work represented much more to her than mere commodity. She seemed to realize she was somehow dealing in her own identity when she sold a painting.

Regardless of her status as a social "outsider" in Sanpete County, some in town respected the woman who painted in her car parked in the ditch beside the road.

Although one Spring City man labeled her "Old Lady Peacock," it took another outsider, an art critic, to see her as "the matriarch of Utah painters."

In all my conversations with Ella, I failed to get her to reflect analytically on her painting style. "I've never tried describing my work. I just do it," she said once. "I guess my style is tonal. It shows a close relationship of one tone to another. A painting can't be all pure color. That wouldn't mean a thing. I was taught to make a tonal painting and to 'make it sing' with a spot of pure color. Then you've got something."

To a degree her work reflects a tonalist approach in its ardent reflection of nature, limited palette, and low-key color harmonies. The colors and values in the open lands, and even the old buildings in central Utah, call for that response. The tonality in her finest paintings replicates the parching heat and dusty air that mute the colors in the western desert. Yet, as is often typical of tonalist work, a hazy, evocative mood in her paintings doesn't dominate the subject matter. She owes as much to the tradition of impressionists who painted *en plein air,* spontaneously capturing the effect of a landscape on location. To work outdoors was a critical part of Ella's experience making art; in that way she accessed the complete environment and replicated it in her images. And, in doing so, she painted the desert's antiquity into her landscapes.

Usually, an artist's style is typified by the artist's era and by dominant painters of the artist's time and place. During the late nineteenth century and early twentieth century, significant colonies of impressionist artists were practicing plein air painting on California's spectacular coast and in its miles of desert. Ella's training, rooted in the Philadelphia art milieu, was dominated by American artists and traditionalists Thomas Eakins and Robert Henri. Both painters were associated with the prominent Pennsylvania Academy of the Fine Arts, though neither man was known primarily for landscape painting.

Eakins was known for his bold brushwork, his "clarity and honesty of perception," and his interest in "painting fact." After studying at the Pennsylvania Academy of the Fine Arts, Henri subsequently taught at the Philadelphia School of Design for Women until just before Ella enrolled. His work reflected a "freedom of spontaneity" that Ella's painting in Utah embodied. He encouraged the large brush strokes she used that suggest a "sense of vigor, direction, speed and fullness." Henri talked about the tactile qualities of brush strokes that are "visible on the canvas" with "size that covers a certain area" and with their "own texture." He approved of "rich, fluid, abundant strokes."[19] While Peacock's style is rooted in the Philadelphia tradition, her final subject and palette matured in the western desert.

Utah artists, collectors, and critics have spoken eloquently and effusively of Ella's stature as a regional painter. Dave Ericson, a Salt Lake City gallery owner who connects deeply with Ella's work, recognized Ella as an anomaly in the community of Utah art. "Ella's a real artist who goes with the flow of inspiration. The purpose in her subject directs the painting's structure. She's almost at one with this desert—that's what I think her paintings are all about. We in Utah don't think about living in the desert. But it was a desert at one time.

"Most artists are so oriented to photos and magazine illustrations that they've never sat outside all day in the hot sun and just stared at something. They don't have a sense really for the environment. Ella goes out there and sits. The sun beats down on her, and she looks at these close color harmonies and just draws with her brush directly what she feels and sees. That's the strength of what she does."

Richard Oman, as senior curator of the Museum of Church History and Art, believed in Ella's "incredible integrity." He said, "She is able to look at that sort of dry, dusty, windswept alkali kind of world of Sanpete County and see the wonderful beauty in it. And she helps you see that. She helps people see the organic unity of land."

The watercolorist Osral Allred, Ella's neighbor, analyzed the lively quality in her work succinctly: "That spot of color she paints punctuates the painting like a flute in an orchestra."

It could be that Ella's lack of analysis of her own work and her lack of interest in marketing it simply reflected the total immersion in it that Ericson referred to. It was evidence as well of her artistic integrity. It seems to me that she took for granted her purpose as an artist just as she assumed the right to her autonomy as a woman. Ella was simply less interested in explaining her paintings than she was in creating them, driven more by an imperative to document the desert on canvas than a wish to make a place for herself in the art world. And, counterintuitive as it seems, she appeared less interested in making a painting than she was in watching the sky or contemplating the sage.

"A bright, sunshiny day," she told me, "takes the color out of things in the landscape. On a gray day you get much more color. Well, I can look at the same place a whole lot of different times, and I can see different things all the time; it is never really the same twice.

"Sometimes I go back to a spot I painted because I want to look at something again. When you look again you don't see things that were there before. But, sometimes I guess I put them together—some things that are there and some things that aren't there. I don't look for a subject; I just look at things until I see something that really hits me. It's the whole composition, the feeling of the thing I like."

As Lee Bennion commented, "She paints what she feels about the landscape. And to me that's what all great art is: you see that painter's soul and feelings. You see Ella's passion for the land—the strength and the wide-open space and the confidence she feels are all very visible. Ella's a westerner; her art says, 'I'm at home here; I love this place.'"

Ella's painting of the Fairview Flour Mill hangs near my desk, its textured volume reminding me daily of the structure's mass. Its cylindrical towers nearly fill the canvas, leaving just enough room for a turbulent sky and purple-shadowed olive-green sage low in the foreground. The painting makes the industrial edifice lovely, its wheat-colored metal surfaces softly rounded. Its plain simplicity shines with the building's character.

I was continually impressed with Ella's determination and drive to create art from that vast landscape. She amazed me really, this woman who had little inner confidence and many doubts, yet who refused easy reassurance where so many of us find it—in fashion, in pleasing others and playing by the rules. Instead, she shaped a new and meaningful alternative life.

It took time, I knew, to appreciate an Ella Peacock painting, to slow down completely to see the honesty that she captured. And I was learning that it took the same kind of patience to understand Sanpete County. Slowing down was something I had to relearn every time I visited, every time I entered this lonely, lovely place.

That night, I slept upstairs in the Paulsens' converted coal house with the windows at each peak of the roof open for cross-ventilation. As I lay in bed, waiting for my mind to clear from the day's discoveries, I contrasted Ella's endurance and steadfastness in her marriage to Bill to the failing hope and faith that had ultimately caused me to end my marriage.

Whereas Bill, as Ella claimed, "brought her to life," life was what had—early on—gone missing from my marriage. While its finish, three years previous to that summer, was deeply painful for everyone concerned, it afforded a necessary though troubled release for me.

In leaving the relationship, I felt I had denied the solidity of marriages recorded in my maternal grandmother's old, brittle genealogy chart, made meaningless my own wedding album, and darkened the hopeful snapshots of our growing family. I surprised and disappointed my friends and neighbors and challenged the patriarchy in family and church. But, without doubt, my resolution to leave saddened my children and marked their lives the most. I had kept my marriage vows to endure through sickness and health; I failed, however, to submit to the loss of my sense of self.

I still often felt a nudge of guilt, but the years of growing freedom and autonomy encouraged an emotional ease I'd not known in decades. At first I kept my astonishing happiness secret, fearful it would be misunderstood by my married friends. Even though my future was suddenly formless, a new and gripping inner sense of balance helped assure me I'd made the right decision. At the same time, I was slowly finding that I could sustain an honest identity in the world and that my work on Ella's story had become a refuge of renewed purpose.

That night as a windstorm barreled through the upstairs windows, I listened to a rusty weather vane on one of the old outbuildings spinning on and off for hours until I finally fell into a deep sleep.

The Manti Temple. OIL, 16″ X 20″. COURTESY OF ROSELLE ANDERSON HAMBLIN.

THE MANTI TEMPLE

*If we have the habit of freedom and the courage to write
exactly what we think, if we face the fact . . . that there is no arm
to cling to, but that we go alone and that our relation is to the
world of reality and not only to the world of men and women,
then the opportunity will come.*
—Virginia Woolf, *A Room of One's Own*

"I THINK I'VE PAINTED my last temple painting," Ella told me often. "I just don't think I can do another." She had more requests to paint the nearby Manti Temple than any other subject. But Ella preferred to work when and where she wanted, motivated by something in which only she could see possibility—usually a particular mood of the sky or the gnarled shape of a sage bush. She was uncomfortable with the responsibility of accepting a commission and especially uneasy with the burden of someone else's expectations. But if she agreed to paint a particular subject, she took to the task with serious determination.

I also read, in her ambivalence about painting the temple, a conflict between duty to her community of faith and duty to herself, to her deeply ingrained need for self-determination. Yet she continually agreed to paint the temple "one more time" for this friend or that new acquaintance. Thus, during the twenty years she lived within a seventeen-mile drive of Manti, she had painted the temple in all seasons and at all times of day. Sometimes the building stood majestic and large in a painting's foreground, sometimes distant and silhouetted against the sinking winter sun.

I was visiting Ella late that summer, and we were taking a drive south on Highway 89 to Manti. After passing the turkey farms scattered along Pigeon Hollow Road on the way out of town, we continued for nine miles, passing large hay and alfalfa fields kept green by huge rolling irrigation sprinklers.

Within a few minutes, we drove along Ephraim's tree-lined Main Street, bordered by old Victorian houses, toward what passed as the downtown—two gas stations on opposite corners, the Malt Shop, the old brick Central Utah Art Center that had been recently converted from a roller mill, then a drugstore and the library. Snow College, according to a sign, was two blocks east.

Seven miles farther on, after passing more open fields, we entered Manti, the Sanpete County seat, our eyes fixed on the stone temple growing larger ahead of us. Massive in its compact proportions, the temple sat serenely distinctive on the hill just east of town as it had since the day of its dedication in 1888.

In the Church of Jesus Christ of Latter-day Saints, the most important rituals and covenants, the most significant ordinances, are performed in temples. Closed to the public and to church members who don't meet the entrance requirements, temples are considered the spiritual heart of Mormon communities.[20]

The Manti Temple is loved as well for its artfulness—its late-nineteenth-century French-revival architecture and its interior murals. Constructed under the vision of Brigham Young and the direction of his successor, John Taylor, in the earliest days of Utah's settlement, the Manti Temple was built by dedicated Mormon pioneers who quarried its cream-colored oolite limestone from the same high hill on which it stands. It endures today as a prominent image revered throughout the Sanpete Valley and, illuminated by floodlights, glows for miles in the clear night skies. When we reached the temple, I pulled over and stopped across the road under the shade of some black oaks by the pioneer-era cemetery.

Ella could hardly contain herself. "That green grass does not belong at the temple," she sputtered. "That makes me mad. Have you seen the painting I did for Lee Bennion, just a little silhouette of the temple? See how they've cultivated the hill, the slope this side of it, that slope that's facing you? See how they've planted little baby trees all over it?

"That spoils the composition—those evergreen trees against the desert mountain background. They need this open place looking right toward you—not watered and planted with grass. It *was* just wild. Now it's all bright green. It's not good."

As a part of the churchwide building boom in the 1970s and 1980s, the Manti Temple grounds underwent renovation. The entrance annex was remodeled, updating the original design—and, significantly for Ella, the temple grounds were landscaped. She objected to these changes, and during the years she lived in Spring City, Ella nearly always painted the Manti Temple as it had originally appeared, as she thought it was meant to be.

Still, the growth and development that had steadily claimed rural open space along Interstate 15 between Ogden and Provo had not yet encroached upon the old communities in Sanpete County along Highway 89. These towns yet resembled the sturdy, self-sustaining nineteenth-century pioneer villages Brigham Young envisioned and Ella saw when she first visited Utah with her mother in 1936.

After we returned to Spring City and settled again on her living room sofa, Ella made lunch for both of us—peanut butter and jelly sandwiches with small glass bottles of ice-cold Coca Cola. The visit to Manti had stirred her, and she began to tell me more about her introduction to Mormon culture.

During the twenty-five years the Peacocks spent in rural Pennsylvania, Ella restlessly dreamed of returning to the desert to paint. In early 1962, in his last semester of high school, Bailey made it clear to his parents that he had no interest in taking over the family dairy farm. His decision freed Ella to redeem the pledge she had made to herself as a young single woman in the 1930s when her long love affair with the desert began.

In January 1962, when she saw a notice in the local Wayne County paper announcing the Mormon missionaries' arrival in town, Ella remembered her earlier exposure to Mormon culture and recognized in it the possibility for a change of direction she felt her family needed. She left messages and a hand-drawn map to their farm at a Laundromat and at an A&P grocery store, noting that she was seeking missionaries to get information about colleges for her son.

Actually, a more grave need seems to have propelled Ella to make large changes in her family life. Always reticent about criticizing her husband, Ella once confessed to me that Bill had begun to drink excessively in the evenings, a means of relaxing after farmwork was finished, "a habit he learned in the army," Ella had reasoned. "You had to be a man, you see? At fifteen he hadn't been old enough to join the army, much less drink, but everybody drank then."

Ella's niece Adelaide, who lived with the Peacocks on their dairy farm for some time as a child and teenager, told me later that Ella had been worried that her eighteen-year-old son would repeat his father's habits or would emulate the alcoholism Ella's family had often called the "Smyth weakness."

Yet Ella told me that afternoon that she had not been sure college would suit Bailey and that, instead, her reason for seeking the Mormon missionaries was "to learn about life in Utah." But years later another niece, Betty, reported that many in the Smyth family believed that Ella wanted to associate her family with the church known for "'taking care of its own' so Bailey would be taken care of." In any case, Ella seems to have seen something formless in her family, something needing outside direction.

Elder Greg Hawkins recorded in his journal that he and Gary Workman, young missionaries from Utah, "were delighted" to hear that a family at a nearby farm was interested in meeting them. Without a phone number, the young men set out in the approximate direction of the dairy farm and found it "fairly close to a very small Catholic monastery." They arrived to find Bill alone on the farm and "tickled pink to see them." Bill told them that his wife had lived "out west with some Mormons for a few days in the 1930s and had been impressed with them."

At their first meeting with the elders, Ella remembered, "I didn't want to be missionaried. I told them I just wanted to talk about localities and colleges for Bailey's sake." However, after their short discussion of higher education in Utah, the Peacocks agreed to weekly meetings with the Mormon elders beginning in February 1962 to learn more about the LDS Church and its doctrine. "Bill and I were both interested but never talked it over," Ella recalled. "I knew right away when I heard the lessons that I wanted to join the church. It really made sense—the preexistence in the spirit world and the plan of salvation. See, we never talked about those things in the Methodist Church."

For Ella, then, Mormonism must have spoken to her pervading need to manage her own life. The Peacocks started practicing the Mormon code of health—abstinence from smoking and drinking alcohol or coffee—and, within less than a few weeks, agreed to baptism. "We joined the church, and Bill never touched a drop after that, by golly. He thought it was as easy as pie. I had more trouble giving up smoking than he did. Boy, I had a tough time. I dreamed about smoking for some time." And, despite a childhood spent at her grandfather's ministerial knee, Ella realized, "I began to understand the Bible in ways I never had before."

On Sunday, February 25, just three weeks after their first formal meeting with the missionaries, and after attending services only once, Bill, sixty-three, and Ella Peacock, fifty-seven, were baptized into the Church of Jesus Christ of Latter-day Saints in the Scranton, Pennsylvania, ward. This new chapter in their lives was marked by alacrity in more than one way: running late from completing their farm chores before the ceremony, they picked up a speeding ticket on the way to the church.

It wasn't easy aligning some ways of the Mormon Church with the Philadelphia-bred artist and her English husband, but they made it work for themselves and their son. Lay members of the church are expected to teach when asked to do so, and Ella tried. But the role of Sunday-school teacher was a discomforting one, requiring her to assume a mantle of knowledge—a practice Ella usually avoided under any circumstance. The experience probably reminded Ella of her frustration trying to teach art in the 1930s. She claimed again, "I'm not a teacher; that's for sure!"

Ella didn't take readily to membership in the Mormon women's organization, the Relief Society. She remembered, "I had thought the Methodist Church women's organization was the cooking and baking club and expected that Relief Society might be different, but it's too much of that, too. I didn't go for Relief Society very much; I still don't. It isn't necessary." And this more or less exemplified the niche Ella carved for herself inside the church and the adaptation for herself she demanded from it.

When the Peacocks moved into their Spring City home in 1970, they brought with them their own take on Mormonism. According to Ella's next-door neighbor Osral Allred, then the bishop of their ward, the Peacocks brought "a breath of fresh air" to the town. Although they often traveled around the state in their Airstream trailer, they readily contributed their talents to their new spiritual community. When the Spring City chapel, built in 1902, was remodeled soon after they moved there, Ella worked on the interior, varnishing the woodwork and patching up holes in the stonework while Bill assisted Claude Accord with the finish carpentry on the Gothic-revival staircase.

After the restoration was complete, Ella sat in the field across from the chapel to create the drawing she used as the basis of a linoleum-cut block print, *Spring City Chapel*. Hand-printed on her antique letter press, the eight-by-twelve-inch image has an antiquated quality, common to printmaking and to all her work, that resonates with the style of the Arts and Crafts ideals. In the print the chapel's stone steeple rises high above the distant western hills, regally tall against a cloud-strewn sky, just the sort Ella loved.

She later made a painting of the Mormon chapel in the old pioneer-era town of Eureka. Its warm hues and bird's-eye perspective place it as an early painting, probably done before Bill died in 1978. Trees in full leaf shade brick chimneys on charcoal rooftops of homes clustered around the church steeple at the town's center, creating a peaceful small-town American scene.

Ella participated personally in church services when Bill was alive. After that, as her hearing began to fail and her loneliness increase, she stayed home on Sunday mornings, her solitude more suiting her than the bustling social activity of a Mormon ward.

I was pensive when I left Ella's house late that afternoon. Since my divorce, I had been contentedly living alone for four years, still peripherally involved in church activity but questioning my place in Mormonism more and more often—which seemed ironic, as I was then close to the age Ella was when she had sought out the LDS Church.

The day was winding down in Spring City. Tractors cooled outside plowed fields, ranchers walked away from finished chores, and some families gathered for dinner at picnic tables under the shade of huge cottonwood trees in their front yards. I parked the car in front of the small log cabin I was staying in, left my tape recorder and notebook inside, and set off on my daily walk to the Spring City cemetery, a mile away, toward the hills to the west.

It felt good to be moving in the open. The simple smell of cut grain and the ordinary sight of penned sheep seemed to ground me. And, as always when I'm walking in wide-open spaces, my rattled thoughts calmed down steadily. Occasional traffic buzzed along Highway 89 in the distance; turkey vultures gyred above open fields. I stopped to watch a snake cross the road in front of me. As it slithered noiselessly into weeds of the borrow ditch, I thought of a story about rattlesnakes that had crept into Zion's Camp in Missouri in 1834. The church founder, Joseph Smith, had gathered with a large group of men he was leading on a thousand-mile march from Ohio to Missouri to provide aid to persecuted church members. He ordered the men not to kill the snakes but, out of reverence for life, to carry them on long sticks across the creek so they couldn't return.

Traversing the cemetery, I passed a prominent stone marking the grave of Orson Hyde, the church apostle Brigham Young sent to Sanpete County to serve as the spiritual leader of the area. Many gravestones identified generations of Allreds who were descendants of the founding family of Spring City. I lingered in front of stone angels praying over the graves of children who had died in infancy.

Finally, on the western-most edge of the cemetery, I came to Bill Peacock's grave. Bill was interred at the foot of a small pine tree Ella had planted, his place distinctive with a cylindrical grave marker Joe Bennion had thrown and stamped with Bill's name and dates. He faced east, ready—according to Mormon belief—to rise and face Christ in the Resurrection.

That summer I'd been watching the stages of a hay harvest in a huge field next to the cemetery during my walks—dynamic performance art of industry. In the beginning I watched the alfalfa bending in the breeze, sensuously whispering under the thick cumulous clouds. A few days later it lay cut, its undulations flattened and piled in rows.

Soon after, I watched as a mother and daughter carefully steered a baler along rows while nearly perfect spring-green bales slid out the back. That day, flaxen bales punctuated the field at regular intervals, waiting to be gathered for winter storage, patient as the generations of former residents quiescent in the adjacent Spring City cemetery.

I arrived back at the cabin to see a couple with an adult daughter unloading suitcases and groceries from their car. It turned out that the property owner had mistakenly double-booked her cabins for two days of my stay, but it didn't take us long to agree on a solution: I would share the kitchen in their cabin and they the bath in mine, not ideal but certainly feasible.

That Friday night, the sun lowering behind the western hills, the Spiegel family invited me to join them as they welcomed the Jewish Sabbath. The four of us sat around an old picnic table in the yard between the cabins, while their daughter prepared candles for lighting.

She prayed in Hebrew, gesturing gracefully with her bare arms, Queen Shabbat's ancient movements encouraging the spirit, bringing all of us into the essence of an ancient prayer.

Mr. Spiegel and I sat for an hour after eating talking about Judaism and listening to the sounds of the day ending. We watched the daylight fade into lavender as a crescent moon rose in the sky, like a sliver of a synagogue's dome in ancient Israel. He told me about the long hours Jews spend discussing their beliefs—contending with each other and arguing points of doctrine—and he welcomed my questions.

I don't remember the details of our exchange, but I well remember his comfort with my curiosity and his ease with his own questions about his faith. I remarked that in Mormon culture members seldom discussed doctrine below surface meanings. We were discouraged from "questioning the mysteries," dissuaded from disagreeing with doctrine, and virtually forbidden from challenging patriarchal leadership.

That night I carried a mattress outside to the porch, wanting cool air and starlight. But the noises of nearby farm animals and my stirred-up mind kept me awake for hours. I thought about the person I'd been for so long and my growing pleasure in my new independence. I noticed how comfortable I felt without the faith's usual restrictions nagging at me. I was relaxed with the tranquillity of feeling momentarily free of guilt for my contentment, for leaving my marriage, for wondering about my faith.

◈ ◈ ◈

On Wednesday afternoon that week, after no answer at her front door, I walked to the back of the house to see if Ella's car was in the garage. Through the screen door, I could see her preoccupied with something at her kitchen table, absorbed in the papers that always cluttered its surface; some she kept in her metal lockbox, others in the table's drawer. I called to her before walking in. She was looking for the deed to her house, she said, but her examination of a collection of old letters, documents, and newspaper clippings was proving irresistible to her: this was going to take some time.

While I waited, I perused her distinctly lived-in space that was less than a kitchen and more like an extension of her studio. The corner alcove where she carved her frames was cluttered with her carving tools, stacks of sugar-pine sticks, and that drippy can of rabbit-skin glue. Her refrigerator door was empty of all adornment save a lifelike plastic cockroach magnet, and her dishes were stacked in an old rubber dish rack set on the drain board, right below a cupboard door ornamented with a rusty horseshoe, a feather "the cat brought in" tucked behind it.

"Here's the letter I wrote to the church a while back," she said, handing me a sheet of binder paper, the text handwritten in pencil. I read it, silently startled at its disclosure. It was a draft of a letter that wholly embodied Ella's personality, showing in print her lively and questioning character as a Mormon woman.

Before I could begin to comment on the letter, she started talking about the early years she and Bill spent in Salt Lake and their efforts acclimating to Utah's dry climate and provincial ways.

When the Peacocks chose to move to the Utah capital in 1963, they carried with them their houseful of colonial furniture and sixty years' worth of East Coast living traditions and attitudes. Based on her previous experiences in the West, Ella must have anticipated an even more relaxed and progressive way of life in Utah. But when her job search commenced in Salt Lake City, Ella's expectations were quickly dismantled.

All the private engineering firms she applied to refused to consider her for employment, despite her nearly thirty years of drafting experience.

"They wouldn't look at a woman draftsman," she said, "and they even told me so." When she asked why, an interviewer at one of the firms told her, "You have to be extra good if you're a woman, and if you're that good, then men don't want you around."

She was outraged. Two years passed before Ella was finally hired for part-time civil service work as an architectural draftsman with the Salt Lake City Veterans Administration Hospital.

"After I'd been there a couple of weeks, I heard my boss tell someone he'd had to take what he could get. So I guess he thought I wasn't any good." But Ella proceeded to score in the top three on her exam for a permanent position and earned two raises and advancements during the three years she worked for the institution. She was sixty years old.

In 1978, when she and Bill were living in Spring City, Ella found an editorial in the church-owned *Deseret News* titled "The Place of Women." It was the height of the controversy surrounding the Equal Rights Amendment (ERA) in Utah and the nation. For the previous two years the church had worked assiduously to prevent its members from voting in favor of the amendment—collecting money and distributing anti-ERA literature in church buildings, allowing speeches during church meetings, and sending Relief Society officers to speak to groups of LDS women throughout the country. Theirs was a concern typical of patriarchal religions: that culturally established and traditional family roles would be disrupted by the ratification of the ERA.

The article described Joseph Smith's advocacy for "liberty for women in the purest sense…to fully express themselves—as mothers, as nurses for the sick, as proponents of high community ideals and as protectors of good morals." Its author went on to ask, "What more can any woman want for herself? What more could any man want for his wife?"[21]

In response to the editorial, Ella had written the letter, the draft of which I now held, and had driven two hours north to the LDS Church headquarters in Salt Lake City to hand deliver it. She hoped to speak to Mark E. Peterson, a General Authority in the church, who she believed wrote the editorial.

I read Ella's letter aloud:

My answer [to what more can any woman want for herself?] is—a lot more. The liberty to engage in the kind of work that she is fitted for and that she wants to do. On moving here from the East I tried to get employment in the kind of work that I had been doing for several years and that was what I was fitted for. I was a senior draftsman [in the East], doing some design work in architectural drafting and also in pressure vessels. No one in Salt Lake City would even consider me, and I was told that a woman would not be hired in that field.

I finally got a job because it was temporary. Was kept on and advanced from there to become an engineering technician. Why was this considered not the "Place of Women"? I wish I had an answer for this. Thank you, hopefully, if you would set my mind at rest on this question.

She took the letter to Salt Lake because she "wanted to have a conversation with Mark E. Peterson," she told me, "to bring things up," but he wasn't available; instead, she was able to talk to only his secretary, who spoke to Ella of "the glorification of womanhood," telling her that "women shouldn't be draftsmen; instead, they should do women's work."

The church responded formally to Ella's letter through Janath R. Cannon, first counselor in the Relief Society, whose two-page letter Ella now presented to me: "I do not know why you were not given a job by the Mormon men to whom you applied back in the 1960s," Cannon wrote. Then she defended the church's objection to the Equal Rights Amendment and its "emphasis on the value of women's unique contributions in childbearing and homemaking." She "enclosed some official Church statements that may be helpful."[22] Ella kept Cannon's letter but never understood these affronts because, as she emphasized that day, "I could have had my choice of three jobs back east."

We sat for hours at her kitchen table that afternoon looking at her memorabilia. One file held what she called "swipes," clippings of news articles, drawings, and photos she'd cut from magazines, scraps of sketches and bits of articles about people she admired. Many of the news clippings were edited with marginalia—her often terse responses to others' ideas as well as pointed corrections to biographical information in reports of her own exhibits.

She showed me two news articles reporting feminist issues in the mid-1970s that underscored her clear belief in the equality of women: one told of Brigham Young University professor Janice L. Tyler's support for the ERA and another of BYU English professor Eloise Bell's concern that at BYU, "women were pushed into areas of Child Development and Family Relations rather than being encouraged in the areas of their interests and abilities."

Another article quoted Brigham Young's belief that "women...should stand behind the country, study law or physics, or become good bookkeepers and be able to...enlarge their sphere of usefulness for the benefit of society at large." Mormons often cite these words as evidence of Young's progressive views. Many Utahns are also proud of the fact that Utah was the third state to grant women's suffrage, believing it an act that demonstrated an early belief in women's rights. Whereas Young *was* an innovative thinker and extraordinary leader, his observance of and push for polygamy can be interpreted only as a model of oppressiveness. Utah's support of women's suffrage was actually a drive to gain voting strength in order to end a territorial government that allowed non-Mormons to rule.

The truth is that it took the Utah Territory half a century's struggle against antipolygamy movements and congressional acts to achieve statehood. It was finally granted in 1896 after the church announced that a revelation from God officially ended polygamy.

But, in the more than one hundred years since Brigham Young made his often-quoted statement in support of women's rights to self-determination, a great deal changed in the culture of the Mormon Church. A huge shift took place after World War II when the missionary efforts of the church increased dramatically and the church began significant growth internationally. At that time the church made critical organizational changes, extensively regimenting its internal structure and, significantly, more clearly distinguishing gender roles for church members. The church redefined the exterior image of the LDS lifestyle, and, abetted by the reach of television, that image of a conservative, patriarchal family has been promoted as an LDS ideal since.

Unlike many of her female contemporaries "born under the covenant" and raised in the Mormon Church, Ella openly objected to practices she perceived as sexist, seemingly without guilt or feelings of anxiety about the consequences. Thus, based on her primary claims to the Mormon tradition that were qualified by her occasional objections, Ella took the safe way to sanctuary. She made it work for herself through compromise: by not wholly participating in church activity in a conventionally Mormon sense, she determined her own place within the church culture.

Without continuing to articulate her resistance to the patriarchy, she simply lived as though she believed in her own worth as a person, someone who painstakingly lived in accord with and documented the plainness and truthfulness of the desert landscape. Instead of perpetuating the social programs of the church, Ella turned to the land, a place unplanted with flags of partisanship and unmarked by loyalty oaths or certificates of worthiness. For the rest of her life she would remain faithful to the church, but resolute in a perspective shaped by nearly sixty years living outside it.

That she wasn't a conventionally religious Mormon was obvious; she didn't speak of her faith in public "testimony," as is the Mormon custom, and she didn't dedicate days and hours each week to church service. She showed her devotion, instead, like many Mormon artists, in her fidelity to the western land, her own golden touchstone. She showed her religious conviction in her unfailing art ethic and in her purposeful endurance to the end, by faithfully returning again and again to the open space she loved, conscientiously investigating its honesty of spirit.

I came to understand that as Ella had sought out the Mormon Church for very practical reasons, I was likewise leaving it. At that point I'd had a long history of faith seeking. By the time I was nine, I had been baptized into two different Protestant denominations—first into the Armenian Congregational Church, then into the Presbyterian Church. The summer I was ten, I was saved, high in the mountains somewhere in southern California at a Fundamentalist Bible camp called Forest Home, completely caught up in the voice and assurance of a soft-spoken man whose neatly manicured hands gently clasped and piously stroked one another, around and about, as he called to us to come forward from the bleachers to claim Jesus.

Though I remained a Presbyterian of record, I also tried the Society of Friends Church as a teenager, thinking that in the minimalism of the Quakers, in a very bright, high-ceilinged room, with the morning sun streaming through tall, clear windows, I would find some meaning.

When I was eighteen and left Southern California for Brigham Young University, it was to fulfill a fantasy of attending college out of state—especially Utah—where I could learn to ski and earn college credit simultaneously.

There I became immediately immersed in all things Mormon, readily forgetting my Presbyterian "pledge" envelopes—empty and curling in their small box. Soon I converted, thinking my third baptism would be the charm, and spent the next four years becoming a fast but never-on-Sunday skier, an occasional student, and, in the end, a Mormon engaged to be married.

Mormonism, the most American of religions, was originally founded in the 1830s by Joseph Smith, a visionary who took good advantage of the religious fever of revivalist times. It is a religion of the westward movement, a manifest destiny for the faithful. It is a creed that teaches optimism and practicality and provides its members with that typical American custom of reinvention through its doctrines of baptism and its temple ordinances. It is a friendly faith that appears, now in the third millennium after Christ, to welcome everyone.

I was initially pulled toward the community in Mormonism, a belief system often described to me as "more of a way of life than a religion." I joined a carefully supportive group of "saints" with comfortable values and familiar hymns, with answers to Protestant mysteries and knowledge of new Scripture. It was a community with an image I admired—wholesome, clean, and dependable. Its members frequently reminded each other of Jesus' advice that "by their fruits ye shall know them" (Matt. 7:20). And they polished that fruit until it shined. Their very goodness legitimated the oddness of the doctrine. Upon baptism, I was completely reinvented and immediately defined. I was eighteen years old.

Critical to acceptance into this community is a profession of belief—a testimony of the truthfulness of the doctrine. Indeed, for a church that distinguishes itself from other religions as "the only true church," such witness becomes requisite, and often routine. Yet, for all the confidence in such a pronouncement, I was always reminded that I should seek personal inspiration and understanding and constantly told I had free agency. But, I was to learn, those gifts of the spirit were seen as legitimate only if they coincided with established doctrine.

The Mormon practice I took to most readily was its industry, its Calvinistic conviction that idle hands are the devil's workshop, that "hoeing to the end of the row" is the only way to live. For thirty years I kept my hands free of idleness (except for many guilty hours spent reading) while I taught others doctrine I had only recently learned, packaged spinach for the poor, and demonstrated bread making, needlepoint, and interior design techniques to the women of the church. I found talents I barely knew I had and refined them for presentation.

Then, when I was nearly fifty years old, I learned who I had become only as I left the world I'd known. Within five years, those same years I knew Ella Peacock in Spring City, I began to travel within and out of the country—around the West, to New York and New England, to the South Pacific, and to a small part of Asia, finally getting far enough away from the strictly Mormon self I'd become in order to find the person I was meant to be.

It was there, walking with friends on Riverside Drive in upper Manhattan, sitting alone in a hot breeze high above the Grand Canyon, stepping carefully around delicate Hindu offerings in Bali, and first seeing the Southern Cross in Polynesia, that I asked questions that weren't answered by my adopted religion. As all the travel agencies promised, my mind was broadened.

Everywhere I went I saw the Mormon missionaries—walking in the night market in Chiang Mai, sweating in long-sleeved white shirts along dirt paths in the Samoan village of Lotofaga, and biking through a shady park in Melbourne. Theirs was an unmistakable image infused with the conviction that they undeniably represented "the only true church." And it was that image that finally spoke to me when I realized it wasn't mine. I had learned it well, worn it, spoken it, and been admired for it. It worked very well for my children. But it was no longer the only truth for me. And like a cautious pioneer with a long stick, I was able to set it aside while remaining still respectful of its earnest intentions.

Once I accepted that the faith's exclusiveness would never be operable in my life, leaving the system of Mormonism followed naturally. I no longer felt split inside, no longer felt my mind colonized by rules and wrongs, no longer felt defined. And once I left the faith, I realized I left all faiths ruled by men who always knew better than I what was right for me.

I left behind the old Armenian priest carrying his incense aloft, left the reverend of the Presbyterian church who later left his wife for the church secretary anyway, left the tall black-robed Quaker preaching sonorously on his pulpit.

Now I wonder why I had been attracted to this patriarchy in the first place. True, I came of age before "the sixties" and spent the "Summer of Love" giving birth. My ignorance of the sexual revolution was caused to some extent by generational and geographical circumstances. But there was something else: my father, my uncles, my older brother, and all those clerics I'd known had power I admired. They spoke with competence and authority, comfortable in their bodies and firm in their clear sense of direction. This was an attraction I suspected Ella shared, an identification with the men who had raised her.

Of course, now I know that the advantages these men enjoyed weren't solely a function of gender or privilege. Power comes, as Ella had discovered, from knowing and honoring ourselves—our own truths.

During the final summer I saw Ella in Spring City, I visited the Manti Temple for what turned out to be my last time. Staring wide-eyed at its interior art, I delighted in the murals that Minerva Teichert painted in 1956 portraying the world's social history with such apparent passion for allegory and narrative that the room can barely contain the work's exuberance. Ella had told me of her first encounter with these murals: "Who painted these?" she had asked a temple worker. "Oh, some old lady," he'd replied.

That old lady had filled the walls with arresting images of the natural world, lush in warm ochers and gray-blues. At the apex she'd placed a Native American man, his arms stretched open to the earth's wonders. Teichert's style and technique, echoed in Ella's broad brush strokes and thin application of paint, though much larger in scale, embraced the Mormon story as Ella's did Utah's landscape, their work similarly imbued with the passionate courage each woman brought to it.

I still drive by the Manti Temple when I'm in Sanpete County. Its substantive presence—dramatic in the rural land—persists as venerable and consoling. I think about the Teichert murals alive inside the temple, commemorating a pioneer hope for order in a dangerous new world. And I think about Ella's many paintings of the temple's exterior, enduring quietly, holy Scriptures of a kind, testifying to spiritual resonance in an austere western land.

I think of Ella's altarpiece, the linoleum-cut print of the bell tower of the Spring City chapel reflecting an optimistic saint's awe, as though the viewer is looking up in wonder and praise. I think of her painting of the small town of Eureka that encourages the faithful with its church spire pointing heavenward toward a brooding sky. I think of these and of the many, many ways she documented the holy spirit in God's country: the natural cathedrals in venerable mountains, the plaintive choirs of wind in lonely meadows.

Being Demolished. Oil, 18″ x 24″. Courtesy of Joe and Lee Bennion.

BEING DEMOLISHED

It is harder to see than it is to express.
—ROBERT HENRI, *The Art Spirit*

ONE AUTUMN MORNING in her ninety-first year, Ella went out "looking" in Spring City. She drove slowly past an old house not far from hers and saw some workmen removing a stand of beautiful trees and tearing down what she perceived as a "perfectly good adobe house." She immediately rolled down her window and made the "thumbs down" gesture. Within an hour she returned with her paints to make one of her most vivid works, *Being Demolished.*

In it the adobe house has been lovingly rendered, its thick mushroom-colored plaster offset by a sienna-leafed black locust tree that towers behind it. The forlorn, hacked-off trunk of its mate stands at the painting's left margin. In the foreground is a leaning fence, its umber stakes just managing wild clumps of tawny weeds. But destruction is not the point of this painting; rather, it is the glowing patina of the building's age, seen in the thick, creamy plaster reflecting a warm light that speaks, and speaks eloquently, of persistence and pride.

By the time *Being Demolished* was made, Ella was doing all her looking with one eye. Still perceptive about what counted most, she painted with a determination remarkable for her age. Her brush strokes expanded, and the paint thinned; the images appeared subtler, the colors more faded.

In her late eighties probably, Ella's eyes had already been damaged. Sustained exposure to desert sunlight had likely accelerated the normal aging processes that promote cataract growth and impair night and color vision. Three months after her husband's death in 1978, Ella underwent the first of two cataract operations. The doctor failed to warn her not to drive, so she managed the one hundred miles home from Salt Lake the day following surgery with one eye bandaged.

At home, unaware of the precautions she should take, she resumed regular activity—walking her dog, chopping her coal, building her frames—and drove herself to Salt Lake for a checkup four weeks later with one eye still patched. She had an accident on the way, requiring surgery on her nose. After that, her vision started to deteriorate in the eye that had not healed properly, and finally all sight in it was lost.

Yet it was fundamental to her work in Spring City that she go out looking every day. "It's my full-time job, you know," she told me more than once. Ella treasured the calling and spent many hours each week driving throughout the county, back and forth, along Highway 89 and its side roads, simply looking. Her habits of observation were not unusual for artists, but Ella was especially dedicated to hers.

Eventually, though, her failing eyesight encumbered her primary purpose, her self-imposed task. For Ella, to look really meant to watch, to keep watch for changes in the weather, for certain colors, for the mood of the land. Lee Bennion thinks Ella's best work came out of her later years in Sanpete County as her palette faded along with her sharp eyesight. Perhaps all those hours she spent staring at land and sketching quickly with her paintbrush were in a softening impressionistic haze.

Still, her vision and her perception were separate. Speaking about sight, French postimpressionist Pierre Bonnard said, "If people could see and see properly, and see whole, they would all be painters. And it's because people have no idea how to look that they hardly ever understand."[23] Until the end of her days, Ella Peacock was determined to see in that unique way and see fully, regardless of the cost.

One afternoon as we sat on her sofa, she began regaling me with disturbing details of her accident-prone history. While living in Spring City she had rolled and totaled two cars. "Once I was looking at the landscape and slowed down too much, so when I looked back there was this post in front of me and I had to swerve. The car kept going around and went over the edge of the ditch. I was unconscious until someone found me. I woke up when they put me on a stretcher."

Her most notorious accident was out on Pigeon Hollow Road when she simultaneously hit two deer with her car. The hunter who had been tracking the deer came to her rescue, probably secretly impressed with her kill. Her neighbor Osral said, "She gets locked into a thought or an image. I don't know if she can really see through the windshield when that happens."

Still, she drove her car daily. "I sideswiped a car a couple of months ago. I had only looked up a few seconds at the tops of some buildings against the sky. The young woman I hit came right over and bawled me out. Her face was all screwed up. I don't know how she screwed up her face like that. The police were called, and I got a ticket. The policeman asked me if I was wearing a seat belt, and I said, 'No!' So he said that would cost me another ticket and an extra ten dollars."

When she wasn't distracted, Ella was, by all accounts, a speed demon. On a road trip Lee Bennion made with her to Texas, Lee insisted on driving in the cities because Ella drove too fast. A good friend in Salt Lake gave up driving to southern Utah with Ella because of her speeding, so Ella drove alone to paint. Dawn Pheysey, a curator at the BYU Museum of Art, once told me about watching from an upstairs window to be sure Ella found her way out of the parking lot after a visit to leave some paintings with the museum. Dawn was stunned at Ella's driving: "She just peeled out of there, like a teenager."

Her driving was well known in town, and, when she was in her late eighties and early nineties, residents of Spring City would give the determined one-eyed old lady wide berth when they saw her battered gray Chevy heading their way.

Her car enabled her autonomy; it was the force that propelled her productivity. It served to get her around her beloved desert, to get her away from "these four walls when I'm going nuts," and it functioned as her studio. She ordered her car with special nontinted windows so she could see clearly, then proceeded to tint every other space—the dashboard, the steering wheel, the seats and ceilings—with paint splatters.

She loved to paint *en plein air,* but couldn't quite bring herself to paint under the open sky. She simply couldn't work with anyone else around. Setting up an easel outside invited people to stop to watch, so she virtually hid in her car to paint.

More than once, passersby pulled over anyway to see if she needed help. That's when she'd tell them, pointing to her canvas, "Yes, but I don't know if you can help me with *this.*" I brought her a *National Geographic* article about the painter Jamie

Wyeth who sometimes painted out-of-doors, hidden away in a large cardboard box to ensure privacy. She enjoyed the story and told me that her art school instructor George Harding had said she should hang a sign on her back when she was out painting that said, "Get the hell away!"

But the fierce determination that fueled her work was mitigated by the loneliness and discouragement that came to her with age and loss. Without admitting it to others, Ella wrote to her son, Bailey, confessing her fear of aging as early as 1984. She told him how easily she had gotten lost on a recent drive to Salt Lake: "More than once I tried to think which way to go and where it was I was going. Had to actually stop off the road and get my wits together." Yet she drove for another twelve years.

In another letter to Bailey, she told him how hard it was to live alone, but asking for help was too onerous. When Ella wrecked her car on the way to her eye doctor in Salt Lake, she mustered the nerve to ask the bishop of her LDS ward for a loan of one thousand dollars so she could afford to repair her car. She told Bailey that she promised the bishop she would pay it back in six weeks. "He said *no,*" she reported to Bailey. So, during the six weeks while she waited for a savings account to mature, she walked everywhere, even to the grocery store when she needed to, five miles away, sometimes getting picked up along the way, sometimes not.

Though she seldom mentioned her husband, a drive to the cemetery brought out her feelings. Parked in the shade of large cottonwoods, she talked about Bill's death seventeen years earlier, her sense of loss vivid. "He was good for me," she told me. "He knew how to handle me. Now I miss him."

The last summer I visited her, in 1997, Ella told me the same thing she had said six years earlier: "I'm finished here. I'm ready to die." That year, though, she repeated it mournfully nearly every time we talked.

I could see the spunk leaving her, ever so slightly. She didn't sound as blithe on the telephone as she had in earlier years when she would say casually, "I'm going to be in or out. I might be out looking. Check my garage to see if my car's there."

Her sense of righteous indignation, too, was dimming. She no longer wrote outraged letters to the editor of the *Pyramid,* like one she had written a few years earlier. In it she had expressed her irritation at a young woman whose earlier letter complained that no one had stopped on the Sanpete County highway to help her change her tire. "She should know how to change it herself," Ella had written. "That should be required for a driver's license."

But if Ella had lost some of her drive to crusade, she maintained her desire to keep painting. Her last summer in Utah she told me she intended to paint the house at Pigeon Hollow again, "before it falls down," and she wanted to finish another painting of the Spring City chapel that Linda Allred had requested. "I've got permission and the key to get into the corral across the street, but I'm waiting for the leaves to fall so I can see it clearly," she told me.

I missed her wit: the first year I visited her in 1991, she had warned, "You know, if I say something in parenthesis, I forget what I'm saying." Now everything seemed to be in parenthesis, if not erased completely. She told me sheepishly, "Someone came to the door the other day with one hundred dollars and said she owed me another hundred dollars. I don't know who she is or what painting it is. It's happened before."

After I left her that last summer, I tried to make arrangements, from California, for someone to live with her, maybe an art student attending Snow College in Ephraim, thinking that a housemate might help keep her grounded and alert. But I couldn't make it work out.

I knew she didn't want to lose her driving privileges, and I knew she didn't want to leave Spring City. A few months earlier she had confessed to me that she was driving without a license. "You won't tell on me, will you?" she had asked.

Her entrenched independence was at odds, however, with her desire to fulfill her son's request that she move to Maryland to live with him. For all the years I'd known Ella, she frequently asked me—and Osral and Lee and who else?—whether she should leave Spring City and move in with Bailey. As soon as she asked me, though, she always asserted, "But I couldn't paint there, and I wouldn't have my car."

◆◆◆

Ella was a woman who seemed timeless in the desert. In some way I couldn't articulate, she had become a part of the landscape she loved. It seemed right to me that she should finish out her days there.

But in November 1997 on a painting trip to Ephraim, Ella got confused and could not find her way home to Spring City, nine miles north on the highway.

Bailey came west, this time insisting that his mother return to the East with him. When I heard the news I thought of something Thoreau had said one hundred years earlier: "Eastward I go only by force; but westward I go free."[24]

For two years Ella lived in Gaithersburg, Maryland, with her son and daughter-in-law, Jan, close to Washington, D.C., and within a day's drive of Philadelphia. I called the first month she was there. She barely said a word while I chatted through the empty spaces. I asked if she was painting. "I don't have my car here, you know," she said vacantly. I asked about her work again the next time we spoke. "I feel peculiar," she said quietly. "It's too green here."

Ella's daughter-in-law, Jan, kept in touch with me via e-mail. She told me that Bailey took his mother to nearby Walkersville in Frederick County on Saturdays the spring following her arrival to paint for two hours on a pastoral location he'd decided would be suitable near the grocery store. While Bailey shopped for the weekly groceries, Ella dutifully painted there all spring and summer, working on a single painting, an image of a grassy hill, its colors bleached by the noon sun.

She drifted through her days while Bailey and Jan worked, often disoriented in her son's apartment. Occasionally, neighbors would find her wandering in the woods behind the complex. Within a year Bailey and Jan had to hire a woman to stay with her during the day.

The next spring I got a chance to be on the East Coast and went to Gaithersburg for an evening visit. I took the Red Line to the Shady Grove stop, as Bailey had directed. He picked me up and drove me to their tidy and carefully landscaped complex where the three Peacocks lived in Bailey and Jan's two-bedroom apartment. Its walls were fully decorated with their collection of nature photography—images of bright-green leaves and yellow-winged birds. Bailey told me proudly of their membership in the Squirrel Lovers of America Society and showed me his aviation and Star Trek memorabilia and a reproduction by Jan's favorite artist, Andrew Wyeth. Bailey's hamster was housed in an orange plastic hamster villa that meandered along the kitchen counter.

Ella came out to greet me and seemed to know me. She showed me her bedroom. A vibrant nature print hung on the wall above the bed. I noticed some of her paintings stacked against the wall behind her bedroom door, including the small treasure *First Sight of the Desert*.

Ella wandered around the living room as I sat down. She explained that she had no special place to sit in the apartment. "Sometimes I sit on the sofa, sometimes in Bailey's chair," she said almost to herself. Finally, she settled beside me on the sofa.

From there I saw with relief that two of her paintings were hanging in the kitchen—her *Self-Portrait* and Bailey's copy of *Fairview Flour Mill*. We looked at a catalog I'd brought showing a current exhibit of images of old barns in Sanpete County. I encouraged her to remember places she had painted there. She responded, "Well, we're in Sanpete right now." Later, she drifted to the bedroom where Jan was folding clothes. I heard Ella say, "Why is *she* here?"

After dinner, Ella went directly into the kitchen for her nightly chore washing the dishes. "It gives her something to do," Jan explained.

On the way back to Union Station on the Metro, I remembered something Ella had said the summer before when we were looking at one of her paintings of the old house at Pigeon Hollow.

"It has just gradually gone to pieces. And when the roof goes, then the whole building goes if they don't fix it."

The e-mail messages from Jan became more disturbing in the next few months. She reported that Ella's conversations were increasingly incoherent, except when she talked to their cat. Finally, Jan and Bailey reluctantly admitted Ella to a nursing home because "she needed around-the-clock care." But they worried about her, knowing how nervous it would make Ella to eat her meals with a large number of people.

In fact, Ella didn't like it in the home at all and, within a week, had slapped the face of a nurse who had tried to restrain her. Jan reported that the nurses told of tying Ella into a restraining shirt and then timing how fast she could break free of it. I printed the e-mail messages and read them standing in my quiet kitchen in California after I returned from work. I could only imagine the tormented vacancy in Ella's soul.

Finally, in May 1999, she was admitted to Mariners Health of Bethesda, into the Alzheimer's unit. By then, Jan wrote that she had "lost her dentures, stopped eating, let her hair down and become combative." Although I felt complete despair, I was somehow proud of her and reminded myself of Balzac's proclamation: "a curse on the man who keeps silent in the middle of the desert, believing that there is no one to listen to him."[25]

Spring City Chapel. WOODCUT, 8″ X 12″. COURTESY OF THE UTAH ARTS COUNCIL.

SPRING CITY CHAPEL

But our memory of ourselves, hard earned,
is one of the land's seeds, as a seed
is the memory of the life of its kind in its place,
to pass on into life the knowledge of what has died.
—WENDELL BERRY, "AT A COUNTRY FUNERAL"

THE RESTORED EARLY-1900S COTTAGE I stayed in the next summer borders a wide canal carved through Spring City to provide irrigation for crops and lawns. Lee and Joe Bennion's daughter Louisa and her new husband, Chris, were living in the house, but the Bennions and the newlyweds were rafting the Colorado, off for three weeks this time.

Twice a day, I left my computer to do the chores. I put on my clogs and tramped out past swarms of locusts infesting the county that summer to move the hoses watering the orchard, sure every moment I'd encounter a snake in the hip-high grass. I dreamed three nights in a row of a house flooding until I roused enough to remember that the sound of rushing water came from the canal outside the bedroom window.

At last accustomed to the country sounds and chores, and having established a routine, I was working well, taking breaks only to water the orchard, feed the cat, and monitor the moisture level of the room that held Louisa's concertina. I would usually walk in the evenings, first to the house around the corner that kept miniature horses I liked to visit, then along the canyon road and back toward Main Street, just to pass Ella's empty house standing beside the tall trees, a quiet prompt to my industry.

The phone call came early on the afternoon of June 24, 1999, while I was outside. Ella's son, Bailey, his voice full of purpose, called from Maryland and left the message—Ella had died that morning.

Her death was a relief to me. Ella's suffering in the impersonal quarters of a hospital—her thrashing about against restraints, her indignation at being given help—was all finally over. A year later, when my own mother died after enduring only two weeks of similar suffering, I realized even more the release Ella had experienced that June day.

For years I had feared the possibility that Ella would have to move to Maryland, knowing she would rapidly decline there—both physically and spiritually—in the "too green" East. I was grateful that my second fear, that she would be buried there, was quickly assuaged by Bailey's announcement that he was making arrangements to bring his mother back to Utah to be buried next to his father in the Spring City cemetery.

The next morning, at Dave Ericson's request, I wrote Ella's obituary and e-mailed it to the *Salt Lake Tribune.* That afternoon I drove to the cemetery, where I was surprised to see that Ella's grave had already been dug, the hole covered with a large rectangle of grass, a pile of freshly removed dirt not far away under a wind-break of large cottonwoods. The grave had been newly cut on the north side of the small pine Ella had planted beside Bill's grave. Ella and I had visited the cemetery a number of times and talked about where she would be buried—on the south side of Bill. I'd promised her I'd plant sagebrush to mark her grave, as she had planted the pine for Bill's.

Joe Bennion had long before placed Bill's headstone on one end of a concrete foundation, leaving room on the south end for the eventuality of Ella's headstone. Bill's grave marker, the lidded pot Joe had thrown, had waited on that spot for twenty years for its partner.

The problem with the grave site unsettled me; I felt sure Ella had been betrayed. But perhaps it was just a mix-up; I wanted to consult the city authorities right away to let them know of their mistake. It was important to me that Ella would be set to rest in the right location, that she would not, in the end, be literally displaced.

But I decided to stay a while, to sit down and absorb the warm, dry quiet near the shade of an aged cottonwood tree. Looking up, I noticed a large bird, a hawk perhaps, swooping overhead. One of its feathers dislodged, and drifted nonchalantly down, spearing itself exactly in the pinnacle of the spruce Ella had planted for Bill so many years before.

I knew in that moment that Ella's spirit had integrated completely with the land; I could sense her peace as I sat near the gravelly path that separated the manicured cemetery lawn from the open field nearby where flaxen bales of alfalfa dried in the hot sun. I stayed a while, listening to the breeze rousing the leaves in the cotton-woods and the distant humming of an old tractor stirring up someone's fields.

The rest of that afternoon I spent driving around the countryside, following the roads Ella had covered so often, looking at her favorite landscape anew, seeing her paintings—scaled large and alive—everywhere I turned.

I felt sure that day that Ella had firmly grasped what she'd come west for. She had done what she had intended—tenaciously and purposefully documenting her passion, giving lasting witness to the land's endurance long before she returned to it.

Late that night, as I looked through Louisa and Chris's collection of poetry, I came across a book of Wendell Berry's poetry. I opened the book to "At a Country Funeral." As a poet of the land, Berry would have understood Ella's purpose in the West had he known her:

> We owe the future
>
> the past, the long knowledge
>
> that is the potency of time to come.
>
> That makes of a man's grave a rich furrow.[26]

Four days later I walked into the foyer of the Spring City chapel for Ella's late-morning funeral. As is the Mormon custom, the casket was open for a viewing for an hour prior to the service. I brought a pitcher of Louisa's that her father had made filled with sagebrush branches I'd gathered that morning along Pigeon Hollow Road, a wild bouquet in creamy blue-green blooms and gray buds. I set it close to the casket, away from the other arrangements of carnations and roses, before I finally looked at Ella.

The sudden sense of disconnect that overwhelmed me was tolerable only because I knew Ella had already left, her spirit permeating the wild sagebrush, scattering the sand and rock on Mt. Peacock, her colors already a part of the beaten timbers of the old barns and fences she sought out.

Her glasses—and that owlish, impetuous gaze behind them—were missing. I tried to look past the startling makeup on her face and hands. She wouldn't have recognized, much less approved of, the effect: expertly applied bright-pink lipstick and beauty-shop curls. That artifice, measured against Ella's art and her insistence on authenticity in it and for herself, made me angry, then incredibly sad. Who was the pale woman lying in the expensive casket, wearing not her comfortable khakis and oxford shirt, but the perfectly white dress and robe of temple clothing? Where was the intelligent face I'd come to love, the long, straight gray hair held secure in her customary headband?

Inside the chapel, cool shadows parted as the morning sun sought the ornate interior through tall Gothic windows that reached toward the ceiling. Its rays glanced off the polished dark wood of banisters and balconies carved in an Arts and Crafts manner. Ella's painting of the tawny western hills rested on an easel beside her—the only reminder of the powerful, raw land surrounding the little community.

The organist played sedate and earnest Mormon hymns. Fewer than twenty people gathered in small clumps in the front pews. I sat a bit toward the back, uncomfortable in the emptiness and trying to feel Ella's spirit in the painting.

But I couldn't. What Ella Peacock stood for may have taken on mythological proportions in my mind. I simply couldn't fit my understanding of her life into the proceedings getting under way that morning. My thoughts wandered; my tape recorder hummed faintly on the bench beside me.

David Ericson, an art dealer and Ella's longtime friend, walked up to the podium first. "Seeing was a part of every aspect of Ella's life. Her job was to see, and she kept doing it," he began.

I thought about my drive the previous afternoon. I had gone as far north as Indianola, looking for her painting of the Indianola mailboxes, those ragged red outposts of communication along the road. I had detoured to Millburn then to see the subject of *House in Millburn,* still sturdy and standing on a patch of uncultivated land. I had stopped on the road in front of the Fairview Flour Mill, an extant reminder of humble industry upon the land. After that, I'd visited Mt. Pleasant's Main Street, had passed the wonderful old storefronts, the enduring red- and brown-brick tokens of another era that she had documented. I had sought out the area she painted as *West of Manti,* a spacious landscape without a trace of human life that foregrounded the gentle western hills of Sanpete County.

I had spent hours and miles with the honesty of her adopted desert homeland, with the sagebrush and hard ground, with the wide-open space along Pigeon Hollow Road and its aged homestead—that place Ella had memorialized, the setting of her most frequent contentment.

"It was the physical time she spent working that made Ella's paintings so good," David was saying, "the time seeing and walking and driving and looking and being aware. She found an unpretentious, unassuming view that spoke to her gut."

David reminded the small gathering of Ella's early faith and education, paying tribute to an integrity that compelled Quakers to "keep their windows uncovered, to allow people to see that what is going on inside their homes is the same as what is happening on the outside. How true of Ella and her painting."

When I next returned from my reflections, Ella's neighbor, the art teacher Osral Allred, was already well into his tribute. A Brigham Young University professor had once told him that Ella needed "to be taught how to use color." He smiled. "Ella used color to teach what she saw. That's what art is about. Many people record what they see and just make pictures. Other people record only what they feel but not what they see. Ella recorded what she saw and felt and made a painting."

It was true; she simply lifted God's colors and replicated their honesty purely through the clarity of her passion for them. She didn't romanticize what she saw or felt. She merely honored the untamed land outside herself and the woman inside. As Lee Bennion believed, Ella painted her soul on the canvas—a soul that saw and felt the land's integrity.

The service ended with the organist's postlude, a gentle progression of chords floating us out toward the warm light where I stood for a few minutes looking up to the top of the chapel. I thought about Ella's block print of the steeple, its stark shape slicing upward on the ivory paper she'd handmade, capturing a faithful and abiding optimism.

An hour later, Ella Gillmer Smyth Peacock was buried just south of Bill on the farthest west side of the Spring City cemetery, her ultimate escape from the East to become one with the western landscape. As the small gathering of friends who witnessed her casket's lowering walked away, I tied the bouquet of sage and placed it on top, a complement to the desert's wildness a few feet away.

The Old Homestead at Pigeon Hollow. OIL, 16″ X 20″. COURTESY OF THE ELLA PEACOCK ESTATE.

THE OLD HOMESTEAD
AT PIGEON HOLLOW

As the artist practices his peaceful profession,
he can hold himself aloof from the rabble without the
least danger or damage to his work. He is alone.
He has what the saints sought for in the desert.

—CHILDE HASSAM, correspondence in the papers of the
American Academy of Arts and Letters, Smithsonian Institution

A FEW MONTHS LATER, I found myself at Ella's front door once again. Dave
Ericson, who had purchased Ella's house years before she left it, had offered to
let me stay there for a couple of weeks of solitary writing in early December before I
headed south for the holidays. I'd spent Thanksgiving in Salt Lake and later that
week stopped by his downtown gallery to get the key to Ella's. My friend Liz waited
in her car, its engine running. "It can get pretty lonely down there," Dave said, but I
barely heard him, hurrying off for one last day of antiquing with Liz.

I arrived in Spring City late on a Sunday afternoon. Ella's yard was littered with a
scatter of long, narrow pinecones; the back screen that had always stuck against the
frame resisted my tug.

It was my first visit since Ella died, the first time I was seeing the house as Dave's.
He had warmed up the spaces emptied when Ella left. There was an old pioneer cupboard in the kitchen now, Joe Bennion's pottery on the shelves, Mormon pine chairs
along a wall in Ella's former studio, antique four-poster beds in the attic rooms, and
old blanket chests everywhere.

Many of Ella's belongings remained: the small Sheraton child's table she had used
as an end table to hold her phone and crossword puzzles, her old four-poster mar-

riage bed she had avoided after Bill died, the 1950s bamboo chair usually warmed by her cat, copies of her hand-printed linoleum-cut Christmas cards displayed on an old slant-front pine desk, even her cockroach magnet on the refrigerator. Although Dave had painted the kitchen and reroofed the house, he left the hand-painted frieze untouched as well as the splatters of oil paint on the studio's hardwood floor, evidence of Ella's earthy palette of sage green and warm ocher.

Paintings by contemporary and early Utah artists hung on the walls, including some of Ella's landscapes (one he'd unearthed from the cellar), a painting of the Manti cemetery by Randall Lake, a small watercolor by Mabel Frazer, and a still life of cactus in the moonlight by Lee Bennion.

And most reassuring, seemingly undisturbed in a corner of the studio, was Ella's wooden easel, topped by her brown felt fedora and holding a painting she had started before she left Spring City. Her paint-stained work shirt was tossed across the stool, her paint box and palette nearby—all set as though ready for Ella to stride through the back door from an afternoon painting the Sanpete landscape.

But the garage was empty, her paint-splashed Chevy Nova sold, and the row of theater chairs was missing from the front porch. Gone, too, was Ella's quick wit and self-deprecating humor, an absence as poignant to me as that sharp smell of turpentine and oil paint, scents redolent of her productive life.

I used the kitchen for my writing space, propping her genealogy chart and photos of some of her paintings on the windowsill. I stared frequently at my photo of Ella's landscape *The Old Homestead at Pigeon Hollow,* thinking of the small, decrepit outbuilding she'd painted so often. She regularly revisited it, almost as an obsession, usually saying she wanted to capture it once more "before it falls down." But the small brick building still endured in the middle of a wide field along the road.

I worked steadily my first day there, distracted once by Ella's black cat pouncing on the crackling rust-colored leaves outside the kitchen window. In the afternoon, about twenty sheep moved slowly through town, clumping down Main Street, followed by their ambling herder, the only person I saw all day. The house was a little drafty, as Dave had cautioned, but it wasn't really cold. That night I slept on the sofa, not feeling right about occupying Ella and Bill's bed. Without a television and telephone for distraction, I caught up on a stack of old *New Yorker* magazines and the few decorating magazines I had brought with me. About ten o'clock, snow began to fall.

The next day and the morning following it, I worked continually, until my fingers were too cold to write any longer. The whole time the storm continued, dropping a frozen weight on the black branches of the old trees.

By the second afternoon inside, I knew I needed to get out. I felt an urgent restlessness, and my eyes were tired of the screen and printed page. After warming up my car to melt brown icicles hanging from the fenders, I drove to Ephraim, the heater blasting directly on my feet. The sky was blue again—with that arresting clarity that always surprised me.

Lee Bennion had explained it over an elk-stew dinner we shared the night before: Sanpete County, about one thousand feet higher than Salt Lake, is free from the pollution-generated inversion that obscures the sky and oppresses the Salt Lake landscape. I thought of Ella as I drove, how diligently she had worked to render the cold desolation and the sharp brightness in winter blues and grays.

I was able to do some minor research on-line at the library, read the *Salt Lake Tribune,* and get my e-mail. By then it was late and quickly getting dark. It's just a few miles between Ephraim and Spring City, but it's a forlorn drive along Pigeon Hollow Road where a solitary turkey farm sits back from the road—its long, low buildings strangely lit in the blackness, a melancholic reminder of the approaching holiday. I looked for the abandoned house Ella had painted so often, but it was lost in the darkness. Faint lights shone from a handful of houses remote from each other; clumps of ice clung to scrub oak. The light, dry snow blew over the sagebrush crowded along the fence lines and stuck to burst cattails.

I felt it in the house when I returned that night: a desolate, chilly loneliness—surrounded by darkness, solitary and removed. I scoured the same old *New Yorker* magazines for articles I hadn't finished and listened to the jazz on KUER for three hours. By then I had gotten into the habit of standing on the heat vent in the studio, staring out the window at the empty, inky dark, that night only once interrupted by a pickup truck charging down Main Street.

At eight I retreated from the cold to Ella's marriage bed, hibernating for ten hours under my down comforter. I'd known the satisfaction of living alone and supporting myself for the previous seven years. I liked the idea of practicing independence, but I was beginning to realize I practiced the sort that works best surrounded by lots of conveniences and, above all, within reach of family and friends. The next morning I seriously considered leaving early.

During the years I'd spent coming to know Ella, I had liked thinking that solitude served her needs as it did mine, that it relieved our anxiety about living in a demanding world, that its quiet allowed us to make sense of the world's complexity.

It had seemed to me that Ella *had been* doing what she had always wanted, but living in her space for just a few weeks, I felt the actual density of her independence. All that looking she'd done for the sake of art—how much had been motivated by sheer desperation, by the need to relieve her isolation while still avoiding encounters with people, which were almost as distressing for her?

Perhaps that isolation had enabled her artistic productivity. I suspected now that she didn't paint for the love of it alone, driven as she was by a long tradition of duty and by a genuine need to survive.

As I sat there rereading her letters and my transcriptions of our conversations, I noticed how many times she had told me she didn't think she would "make it through another winter," how many times she asked me if I thought she "should move back east" again, and how frequently she said she was "finished" with this life.

And I noticed how often she talked about money in her letters to Bailey, how fearful she was of depleting her savings account. Once she told him she had recently sold five paintings and said she was proud to be able to build her savings—and in a subsequent letter asked if he thought she had been boastful. In a later letter, she closed with a question, "*Did* I make a mistake by trying to be all powerful and figuring out everything myself? Anyhow, I'm *tired* of it." It was probably in this silent kitchen she wrote those letters.

Maybe it wasn't the cold of the winters as much as the soundless void of the winter nights she dreaded. Perhaps the quiet power so many noticed in her paintings was not entirely a reflection of her forceful, unassuming personality, but a replication of her profound seclusion, her own subtly toned expanse of inner loneliness.

It seems sometimes that the reality of our lives lies in the details between the contradictions, between, in Ella's case, her stubborn insistence on living alone doing what she wanted and the resolve required to outlast her isolation. Some of the truth of her life filled that space between her losses and her persistent intention to document the integrity of the landscape. As I look for that truth in her life story, I return always to look at her art, where she painted herself, the calm authority of her own integrity and spirit.

After the first week living in Ella's house, I began to adjust to the desolation of the Spring City winter: I soon learned to keep an extra pair of shoes on the heat register. I learned to drive very slowly on unplowed streets and to watch for confused deer on Pigeon Hollow Road. I reconciled myself to the local library's limited collection and to connecting with the outside world on-line there. At the house, I worked longer hours, sometimes in bed, writing by hand or using the battery on my laptop early in the mornings and late at night.

One dark evening, standing on the porch before bed, I noticed something, a shift, some nearly imperceptible change in the air. What was it? And then I had it. The smell of the frigid atmosphere was strangely familiar: the promise of more snow on its way. It was nature's inimitable cycle at work, its clues informing us only in quiescence.

When I finally left Spring City, heading south before light one morning, I had to stop twice for deer on Pigeon Hollow Road. First, a yearling appeared who feigned right, then left, as though he wanted to dance with my car; later, a doe suddenly leaped across the road as I approached, just missing certain death, my headlights illuminating her boldness.

First Sight of the Desert. OIL, 12″ X 9″. COURTESY OF THE AUTHOR.

FIRST SIGHT OF THE DESERT

I dwell in Possibility—
A fairer House than Prose—
More Numerous of Windows—
Superior—for doors—
—EMILY DICKINSON, *The Complete Poems of Emily Dickinson*

OVER THE YEARS of my summer visits to Spring City, the potential of owning the small treasure *First Sight of the Desert* took many forms. Once, late in August the second summer I interviewed her, Ella told me she would sell the painting to me someday, indicating, I thought, her trust in my high regard for it.

The next summer, I wished I'd had her write down the pledge and attach it to the back of the painting because she told me that *First Sight of the Desert* would go to the Brigham Young University Museum of Art. I said nothing and hid my sudden jealousy.

Years later, her daughter-in-law, Jan, told me she and Bailey would one day soon sell all the paintings they had brought from Utah after Ella died, all, that is, except the smallest one—"that little one with the blue sage. We'll keep that one because it will fit in the motor home we'll get when we retire." Again, I was silent.

Now I think back to the day I first met Ella. Standing together in her home, we contemplated with respect that extraordinary 1930s document of raw youth. Its nearly virginal turquoise sage and salmon-colored sand recorded her awe—expectant and optimistic.

For twenty-four years, Ella painted the durable plant she had learned to love when she was young, at the end of her days portraying it with her distinctive brush strokes of thin paint in a softer and graver palette. And for ten of those years, the years I was learning her life, my longing grew for that small painting that to me represented the substance and texture of Ella Peacock's self-reliant endurance.

After I'd known her for years, Ella acknowledged her love for the plant I'd also grown to admire, a "trash plant" to many westerners, but remarkable to her: "I like the color and the texture of the sagebrush, the way it grows by itself, shooting off in different directions for no reason. It looks so good next to the warm earth colors. It's wild and goes where it wants."

◆◇◆

When I left my marriage and family home nine years earlier, it was to find myself in the solitude I'd long craved. Like the native oaks growing on the northern California hillsides, I yearned to expand into the space and time I had long believed living alone would give me. Now, within a few years after Ella's death, I'm finally beginning to feel whole, even as I am aware of the implicit complexity wholeness brings.

Without a belief system to provide facile answers that shelve unhappiness, insecurity, and dissatisfaction, I'm left with just a compass for orientation. I'm looking outward, into open space that I realize is saturated with risk, so I can experience more fully an honest reality, so I can learn to accept sporadic loneliness and to embrace the flashes of contentment that come easily when I'm paying close enough attention.

Knowing Ella Peacock has given me a deeper connection to place, to the changing moods of the natural world, a relationship I'd once known but had nearly lost before I met the woman who found her spiritual home in open land where she became herself. And as I travel the landscape, the new geography of my perspective reveals paintings everywhere—in sweeping headlands and salty shores, in leaning palms and massive eucalyptus. A divine, authentic presence surrounds me in the natural world and persists vigorously in my interior landscape.

By leaving the Mormon Church, I have found room enough to become more aware of the divine within and without myself. It's difficult to pay proper attention in the world, but in the attempt, I'm finding myself enlarged by an unexpected openness and more hopeful of possibility.

My experience of this world—in the rocks and currents of its truths, in its cadences and colors—is instructing me to accept the paradox and the wisdom of gathering in and letting go. I'm learning those places where I feel most at home. And I recognize the irony: that the Mormon Church brought me to Utah and to Ella, where I found, only in my leaving, a spiritual arrival.

Despite years of dashed hopes to obtain it, *First Sight of the Desert* hangs in my bedroom today. Bailey and Jan decided to sell it to me after all. Cognizant of the responsibility, and feeling like its temporary guardian, I've carefully placed it on a wall opposite my bed where it gets no direct sunlight. Its canvas is beginning to craze, but the colors remain as brightly pure as when they were painted one day seventy years ago.

I wake up some mornings and lie in bed looking at it, imagining the day Gillmer Smyth made the painting. It must have been a lush spring day following a heavy winter in a meadow somewhere in the seemingly empty expanse of Nevada.

She was probably alone, perhaps the others off hiking or painting elsewhere. She most likely sat on a khaki canvas camp stool or on the running board of her old car to paint, entranced by the expansive wilderness. Gillmer must have been impatient with excitement and afraid, too, as she tried to fit the vast beauty onto such a small canvas. And perhaps that's what I respond to most in it: the courage it took to make the incomprehensible personal and intimate.

I realize the painting was a sort of heirloom for Ella, a reminder of a moment she couldn't replicate—the first time she fell in love.

I'm writing at my desk in northern California, my hot tea fragrant in a cup Joe Bennion made, the arms of his Y-shaped stamp reaching up in praise of a generous God. I look out the window at my favorite trees—a stand of tall, stately eucalyptus, their sage-green elongated leaves graceful in the warm breeze.

A beloved subject for California impressionist artists in the 1920s and 1930s, eucalyptus trees were planted along roads as windbreaks on early California rancheros and are common on the coast where the offshore breeze spreads the spice of their heady scent. Many botanists and environmentalists despise them for their invasiveness and their capacity to fuel wildfires, but I never tire of looking at the considerable outlines they make against a bright sky or at the earth colors they produce, especially the red blossoms some varieties turn out in the spring that sing against their gray-green leaves. California's eucalyptus trees are, conceivably, my sagebrush.

I still visit Utah yearly. Like most places, it's never the same: its cities are dynamic and changing with the times, evolving into their own futures. Spring City has grown some, but much more slowly. Far on the western side of the cemetery, Ella Peacock's headstone stands next to the sagebrush I eventually planted as promised. Two friends helped me dig it up on Pigeon Hollow Road and replant it by her grave. Because the automatic sprinklers give it more water than it wants, it struggles there on the landscaped green.

Within sight, though, the desert's ubiquitous wild sage, that blue-green of Ella's art, remains unyielding—persistent and patient in the landscape.

NOTES

1. Eugene O'Neill, "Mourning Becomes Electra," in *Complete Plays, Volume 2: 1920-1932* (New York: Library of America, 1988), 938.

2. *Los Angeles Times,* 5 January 1886, 2.

3. Germantown Friends School Web site, http://www.gfsnet.org, accessed 14 June 2001.

4. John Berger, "Steps towards a Small Theory of the Visible," in *The Shape of a Pocket* (New York: Pantheon Books), cited in *Harper's* (March 2002): 30.

5. Nina Walls, *Art, Industry, and Women's Education: The Philadelphia School of Design for Women, 1848-1932,* published PhD diss., University of Delaware, 1995, 199; "New Opportunities for an Old Art School," *Art Digest* (1 July 1932): 24.

6. Page Talbott and Patricia Tanis Sydney, "The Philadelphia Ten: A Women's Artist Group," *American Art Review* (January-February 1998): 110.

7. Ibid., 111.

8. Walls, *Art, Industry, and Women's Education,* 207, 227.

9. Theodore C. Knauff, *Training for the Useful and the Beautiful* (Philadelphia: Philadelphia School of Design for Women, 1922), 89.

10. *Design for Women: A History of the Moore College of Art* (Pennsylvania: Livingston Publishing, 1968), 40.

11. Walls, *Art, Industry, and Women's Education,* 357.

12. Ibid., 208.

13. Ibid.

14. F. Scott Fitzgerald, *The Great Gatsby* (New York: Macmillan, 1925), 184.

15. Mary Austin, *The Land of Little Rain* (Boston: Houghton Mifflin, 1903), 1.

16. Mary Morris, *Maiden Voyages* (New York: Random House, 1993), 158.

17. Emily Carr quoted in Sharyn Rohlfsen Udall, *Carr, O'Keeffe, Kahlo* (New Haven: Yale University Press, 2000), 246.

18. Penny L. Perlmutter to Ella Peacock, 28 March 1984, in possession of the author.

19. Daniel M. Mendelowitz, *A History of American Art* (New York: Holt, Rinehart, and Winston, 1960), 314; Robert Henri, *The Art Spirit* (New York: Harper and Row, 1923), 68.

20. Requirements to participate in LDS temple ceremonies include professed allegiance to Christian faith; belief in LDS doctrine and support of patriarchal authority; chastity; consistent church attendance; honesty; full tithe payment; adherence to a code of health that prohibits use of alcohol, coffee, tea, and tobacco; spousal and child support—obligation fulfillment; and consistent wearing of religious undergarments.

21. "The Place of Women," *Deseret News,* 11 March 1978, 16.

22. Janath R. Cannon to Ella Peacock, 12 July 1978, copy of letter in author's possession.

23. Pierre Bonnard, quoted in Sarah Whitfield and John Elderfield, *Bonnard* (New York: Harry N. Abrams, 1998), 17.

24. Henry David Thoreau, "Walking," in *Walden and Other Writings of Henry David Thoreau,* ed. Brooks Atkinson (New York: Modern Library, 1937), 607.

25. Honoré de Balzac, quoted in Whitfield and Elderfield, *Bonnard,* 17.

26. Wendell Berry, *The Selected Poems of Wendell Berry* (Washington, D.C.: Counterpoint, 1998), 91.

ACKNOWLEDGMENTS

IN ORDER TO GET essential distance from my daily life and valuable proximity to Ella's, I needed the many offers of living space in Sanpete County that came regularly and unbidden. I am grateful for the comfort and availability of various sofas, a log cabin, a few cottages, a ranch house, and Ella's old adobe. I send aloha to Tony, my Hawaiian patron, who provided an entire summer of tropical working space.

My writing acquired the grounding it needed in part from Dave Ericson's patience with my countless questions and our long conversations about Utah art. Joe and Lee Bennion's subtle and honest devotion to Ella encouraged my own. I appreciate the generosity of Ella's many relatives all over the country who willingly accommodated my schedule and random curiosity.

I am indebted to my friend Liz, who read the manuscript, endured many trips to Sanpete, dug up sagebrush, listened for years, and easily grasped my passion. And warmth to Al, my own private botanist, who patiently waited and carefully responded.

My editor, Dawn Marano, tirelessly gave me the most prescient advice, carefully teasing my mind around central themes she deciphered in my roughest work.

Most important, I acknowledge my children's indulgence of this decade-long meandering project, especially their understanding of my abiding attraction to Sanpete County.

ABOUT THE AUTHOR

KATHRYN ABAJIAN spent her childhood and youth in Southern California. She has lived in the San Francisco Bay area, where she presently teaches and writes, since the early 1970s. She is the author of travel, memoir, and biographical essays. This is her first book.